Lilah Raizel

Dark Journey

Lilah Raizel: Dark Journey

The Merry Blacksmith Studio
70 Lenox Ave.
West Warwick, RI 02893

merryblacksmith.com
merryblacksmithstudio.com
merryblacksmithshop.com

Published in the USA by The Merry Blacksmith Studio

ISBN—1-51521-384-6
978-1-51521-384-0

Naked came I, naked shall I go
Just without anything else,
Naked came I, naked shall I go
With nothing but naked.

Deprived of, bereft of anything
I shall go, I shall go
Bereft of anything else,
You say it what is my own here?

– Bijay Kant Dubey
"Naked Came I, Naked I Shall Go"

She calls and says, "I was thrown over a jump while riding a couple of days ago and I am pretty banged up."

"No worries," he says, "we'll shoot in black and white, and go for a dark, macabre feel."

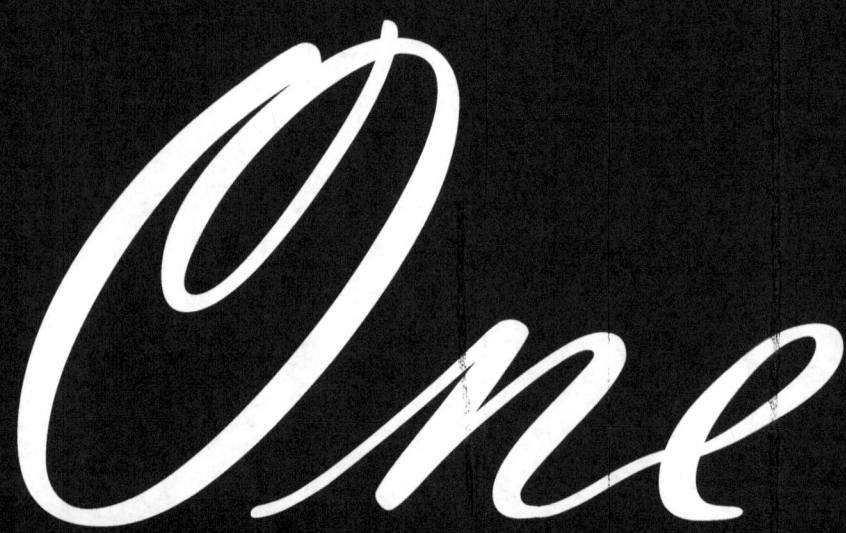

One

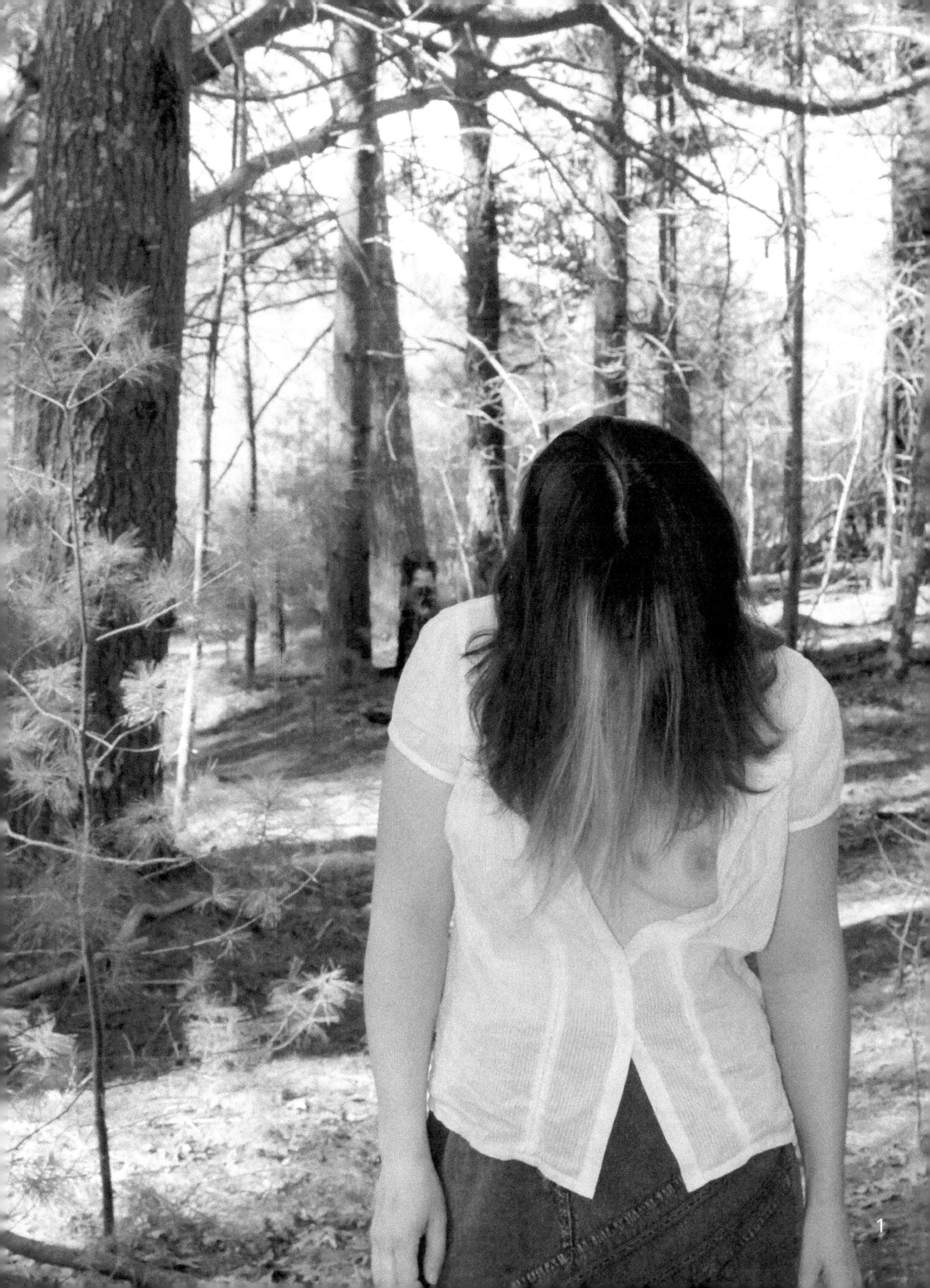

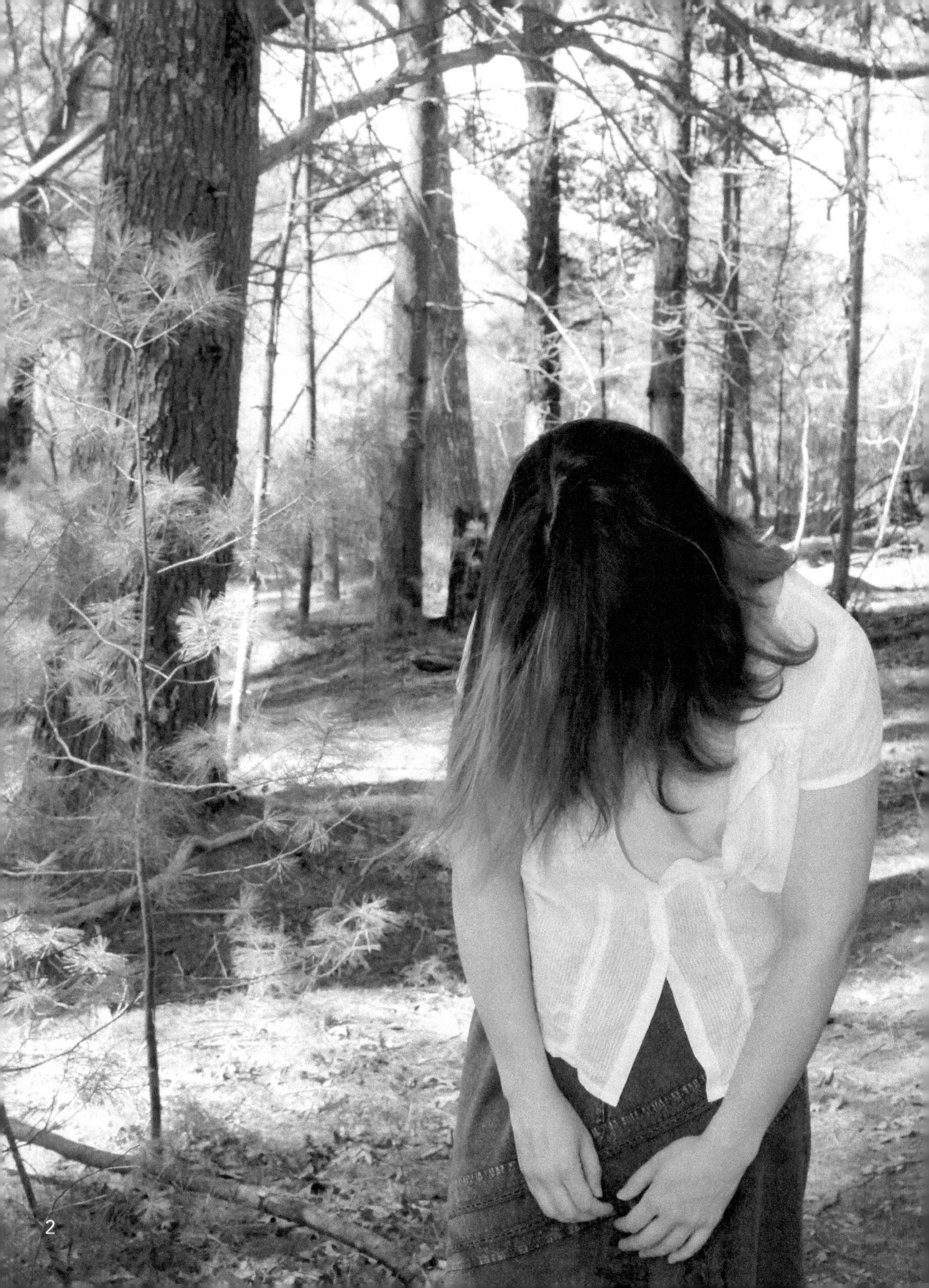

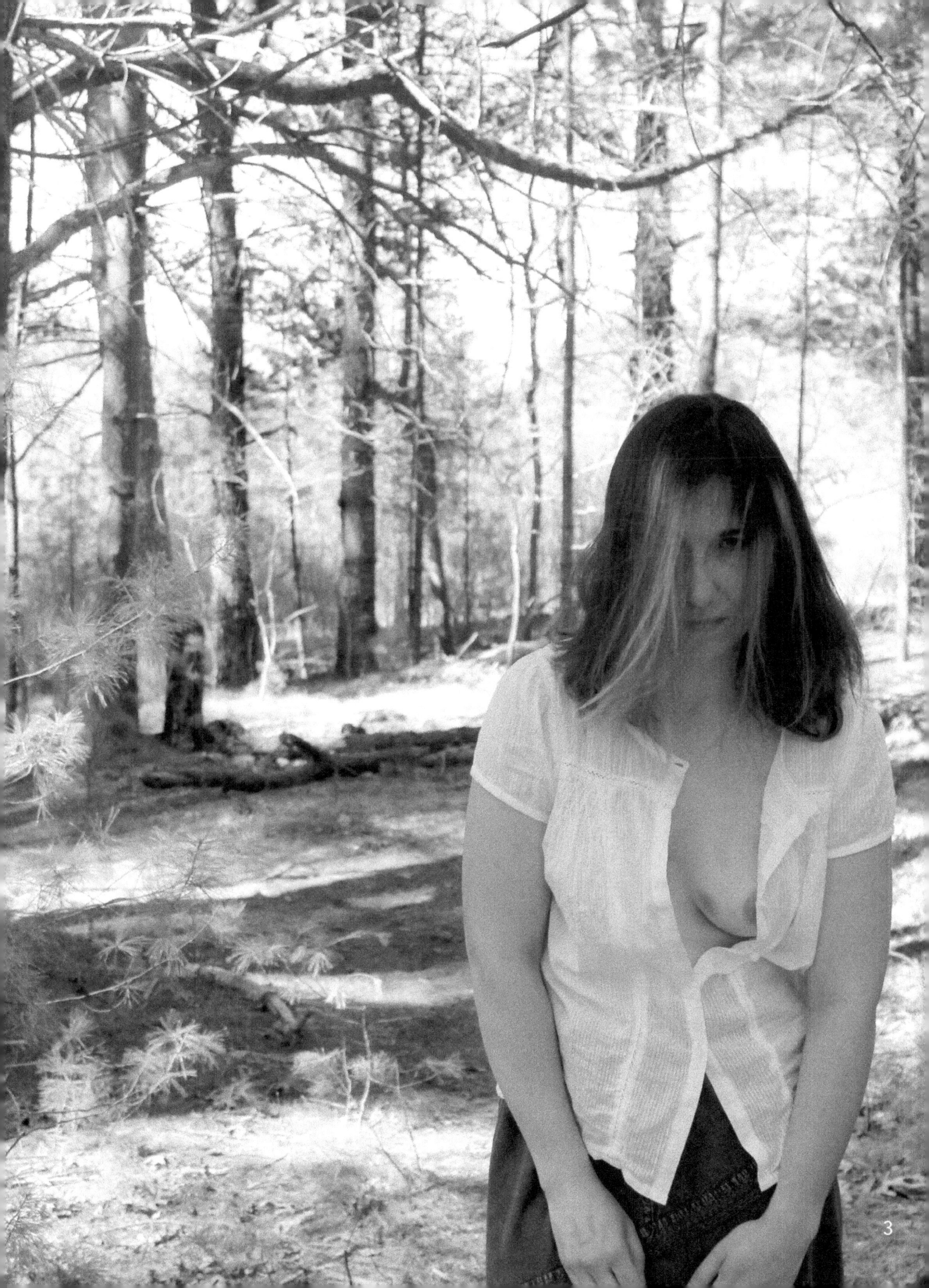

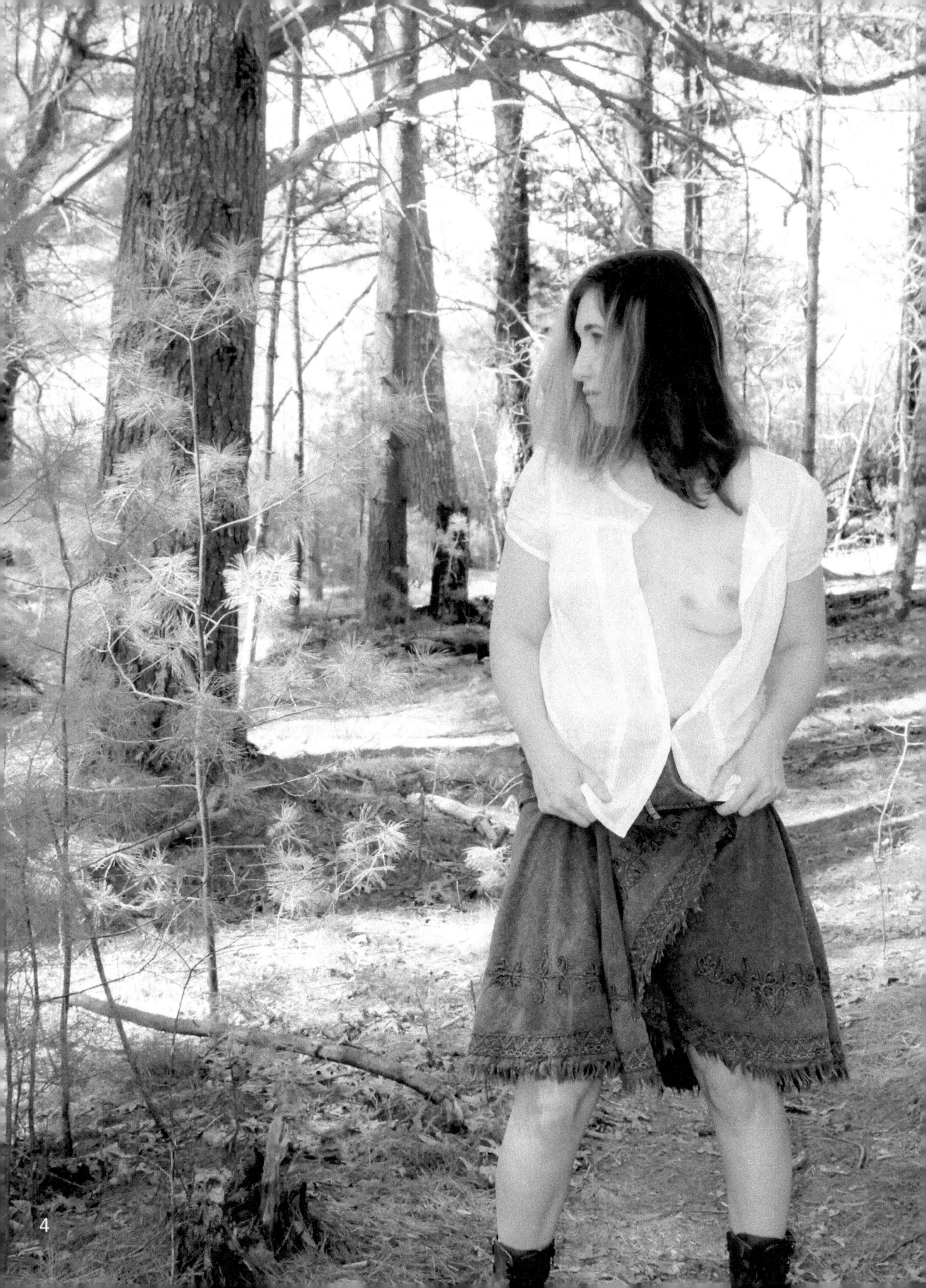

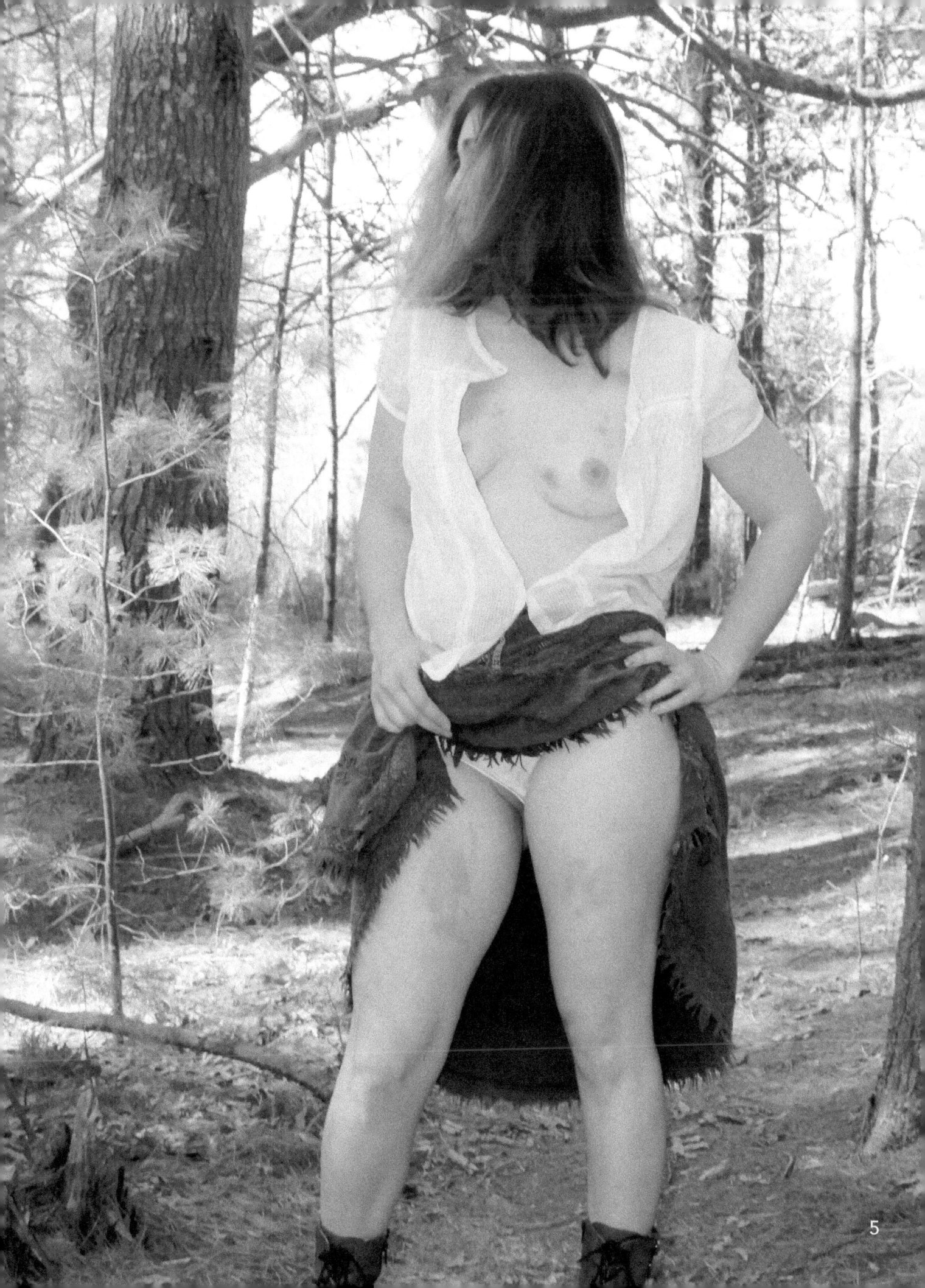

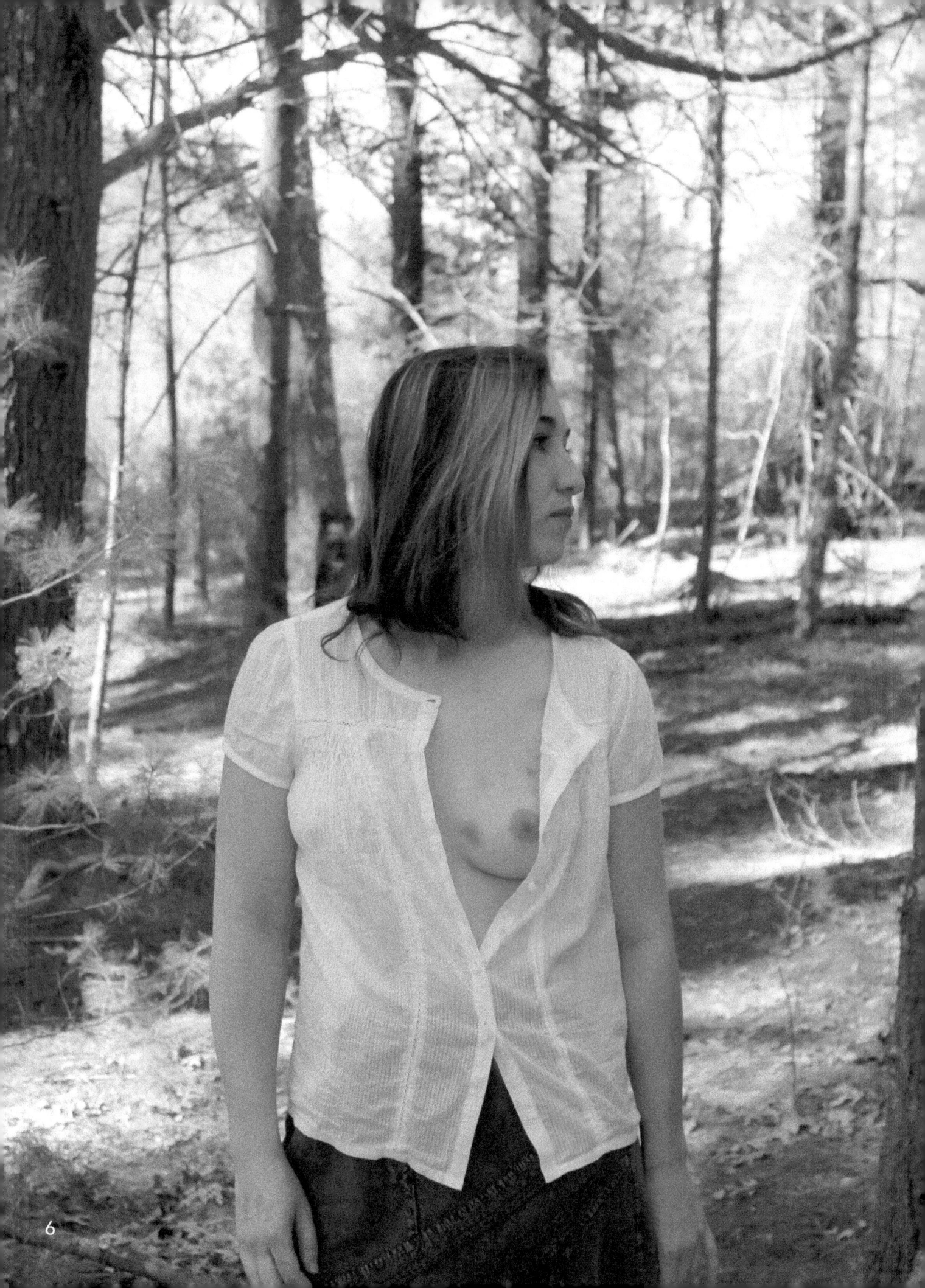

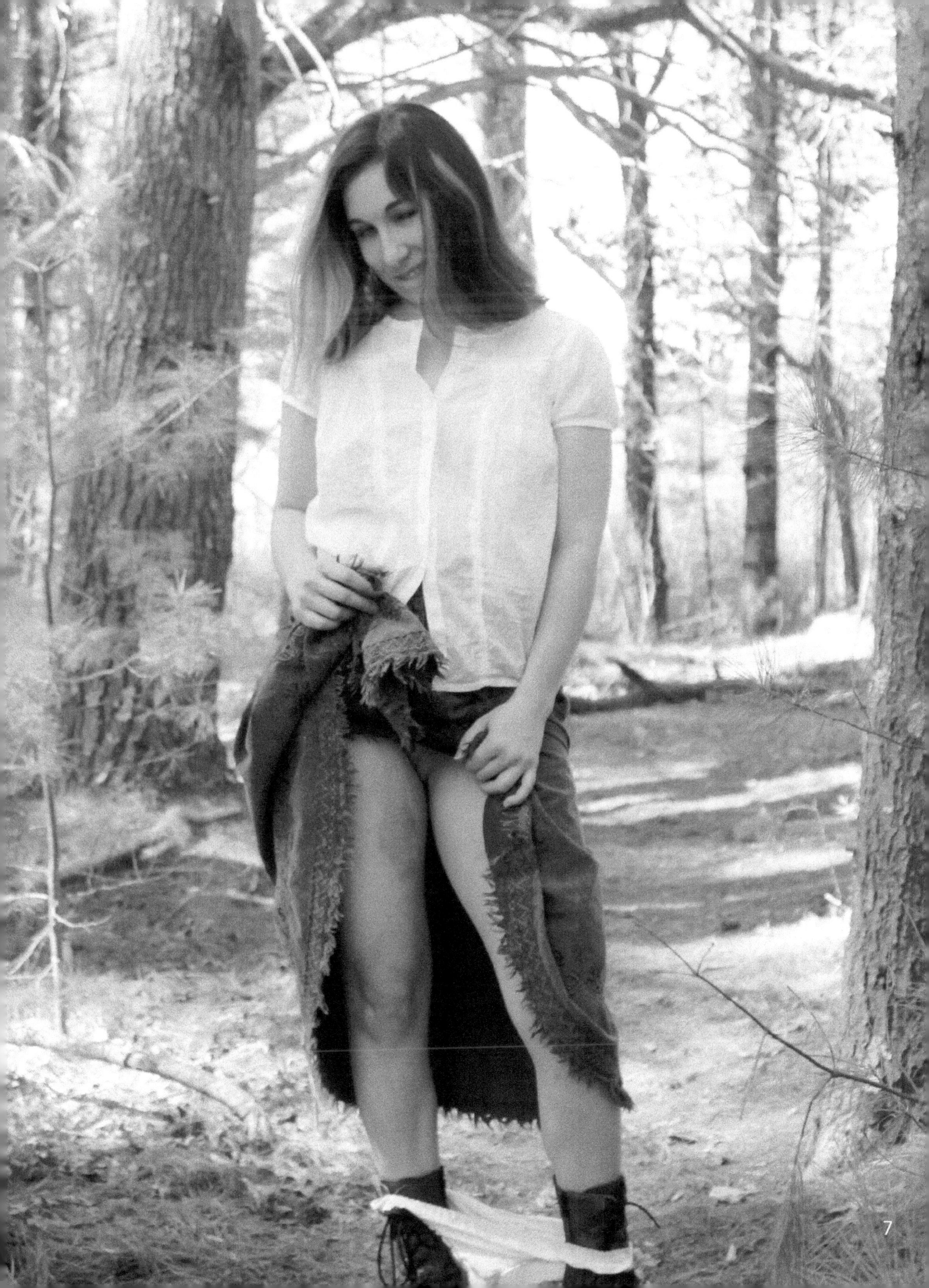

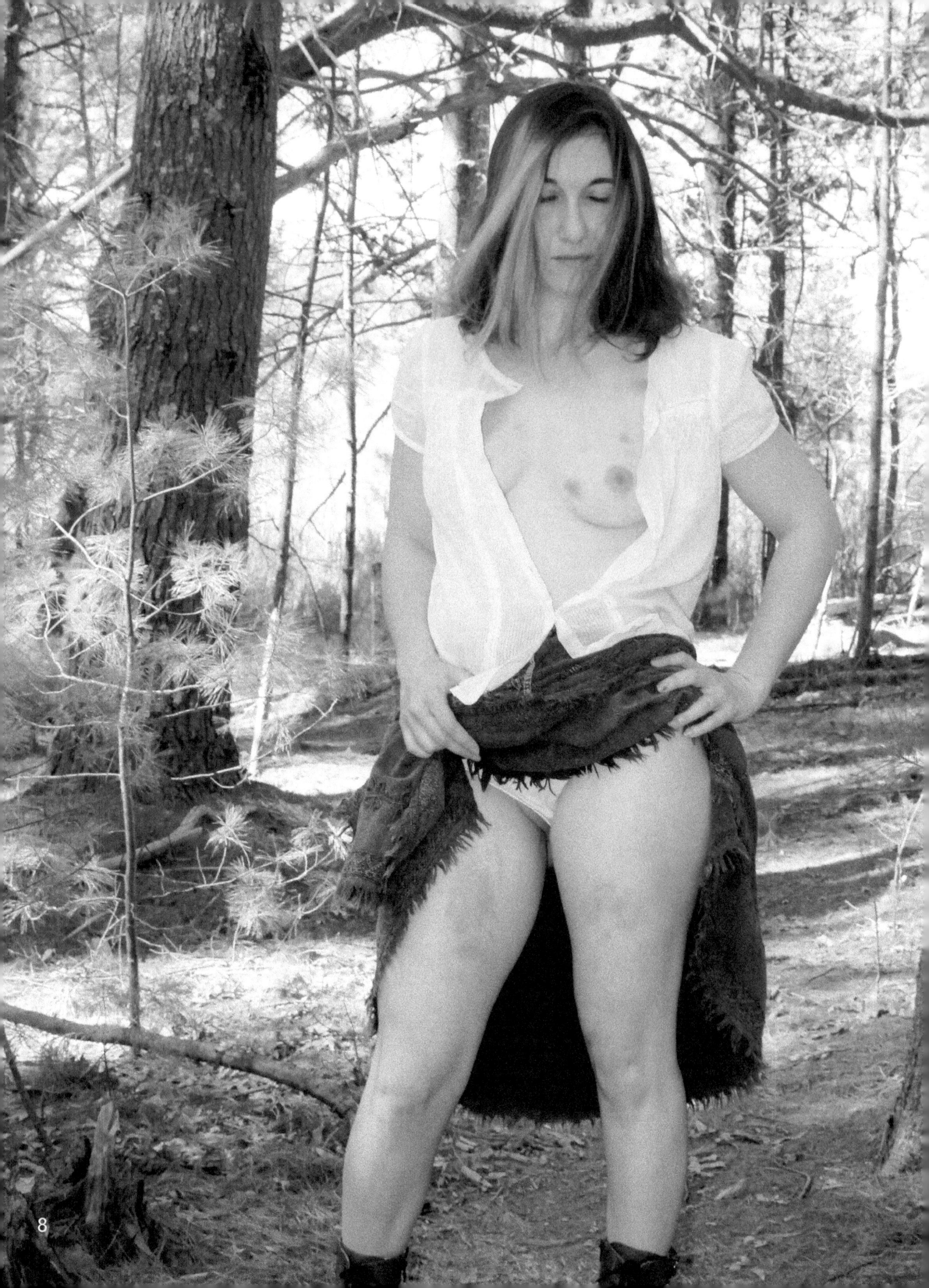

8

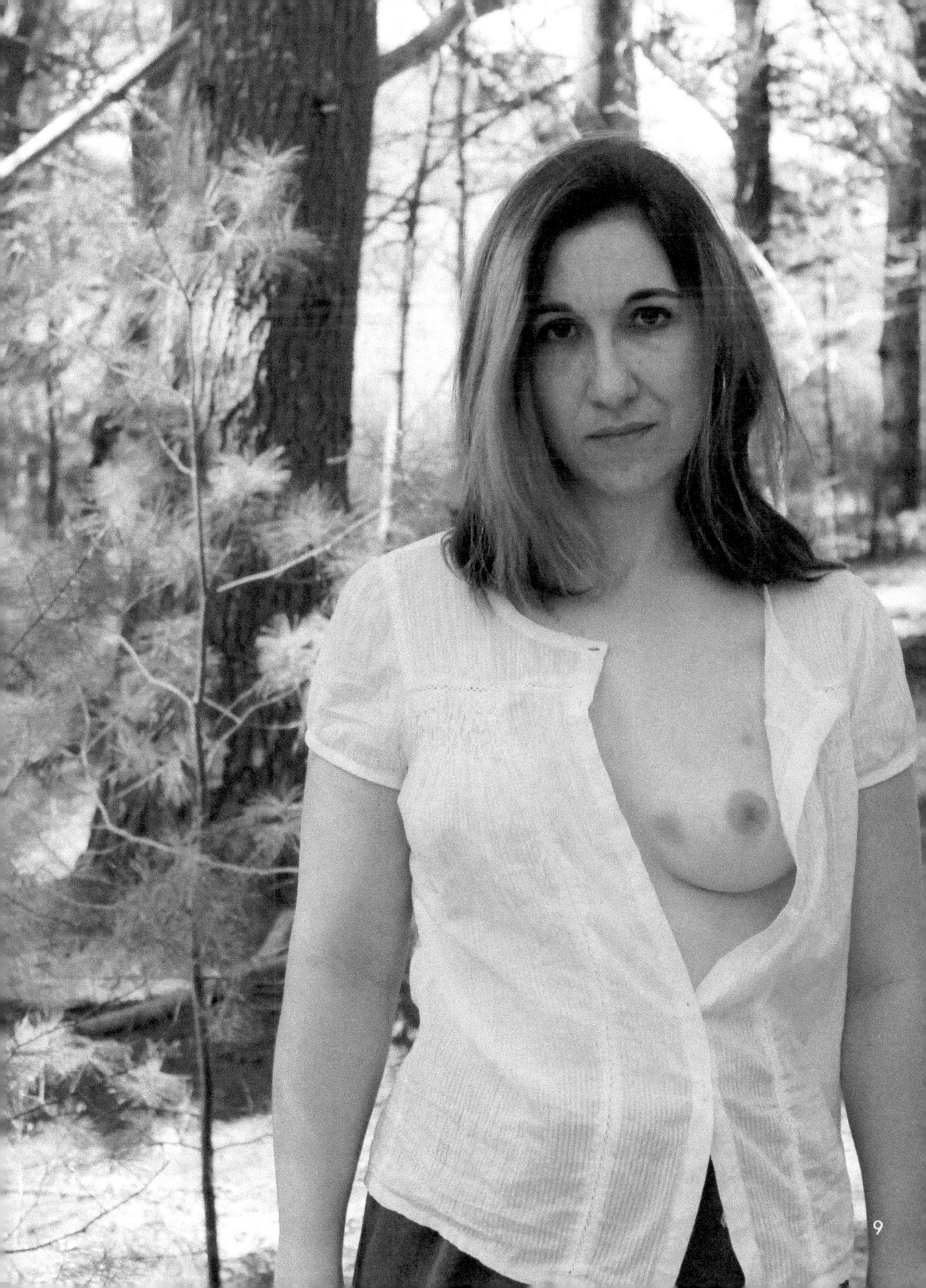

"I think that it is those
who see the most
that are oft-times
the most blind."

Two

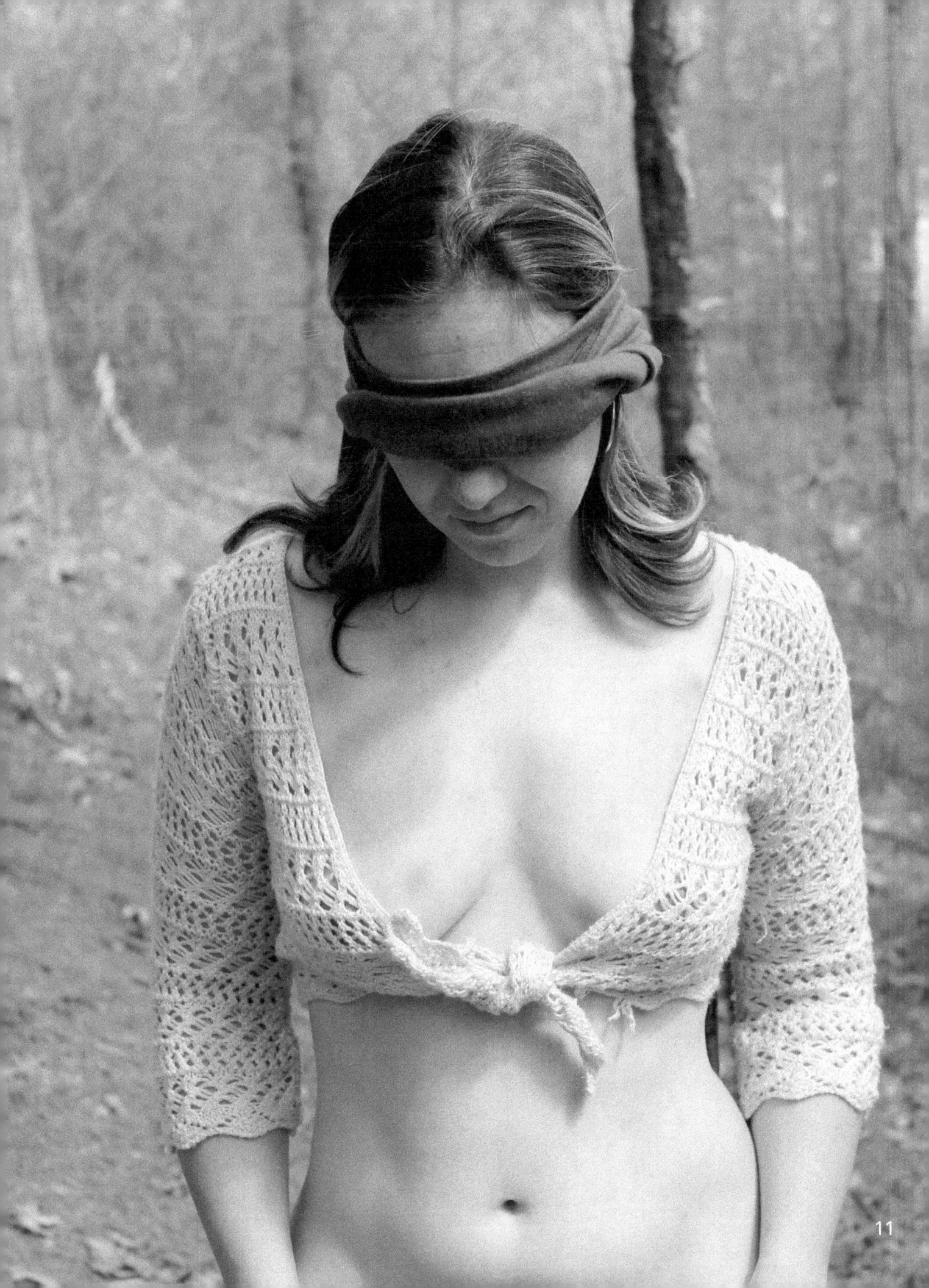

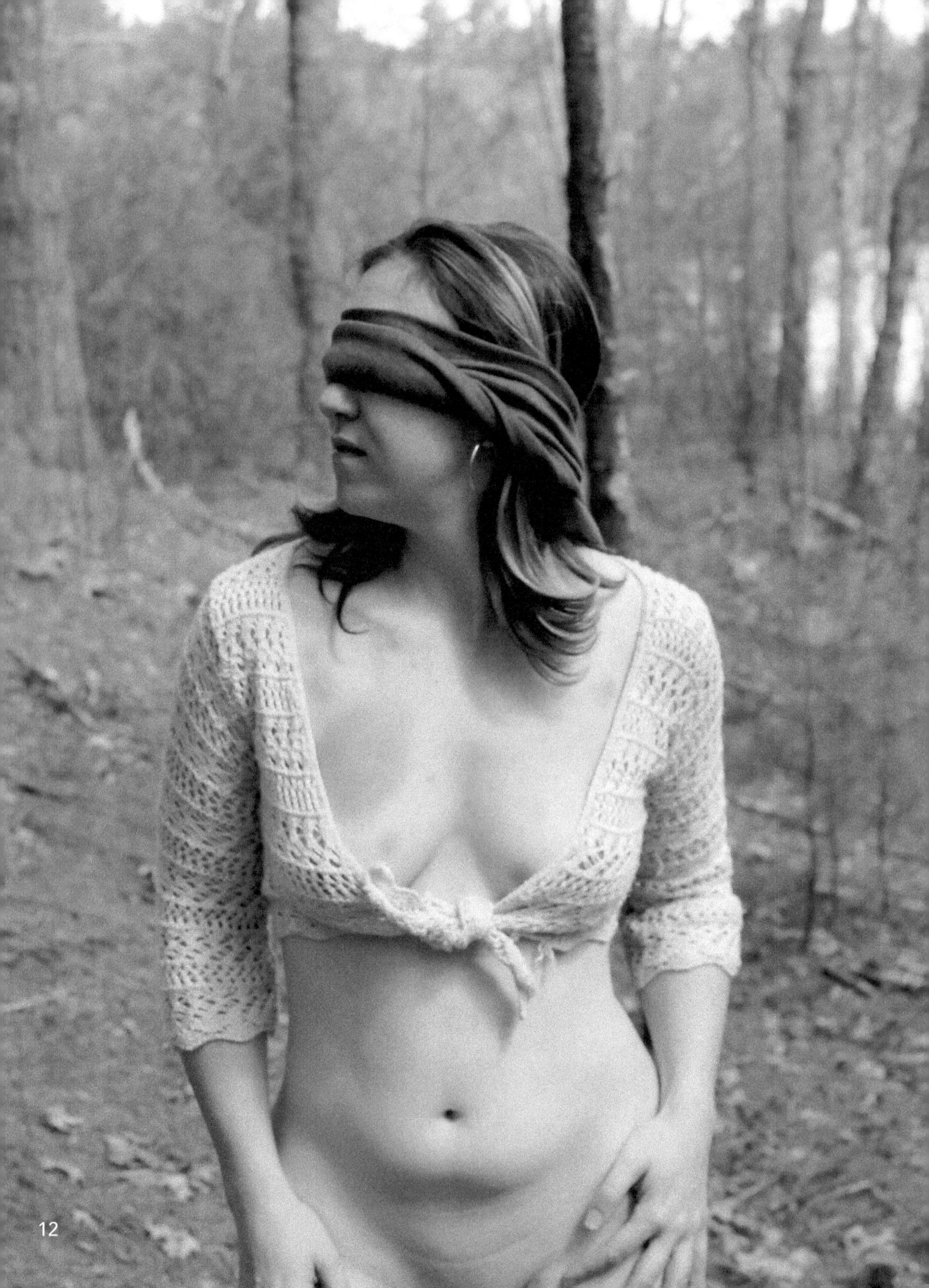

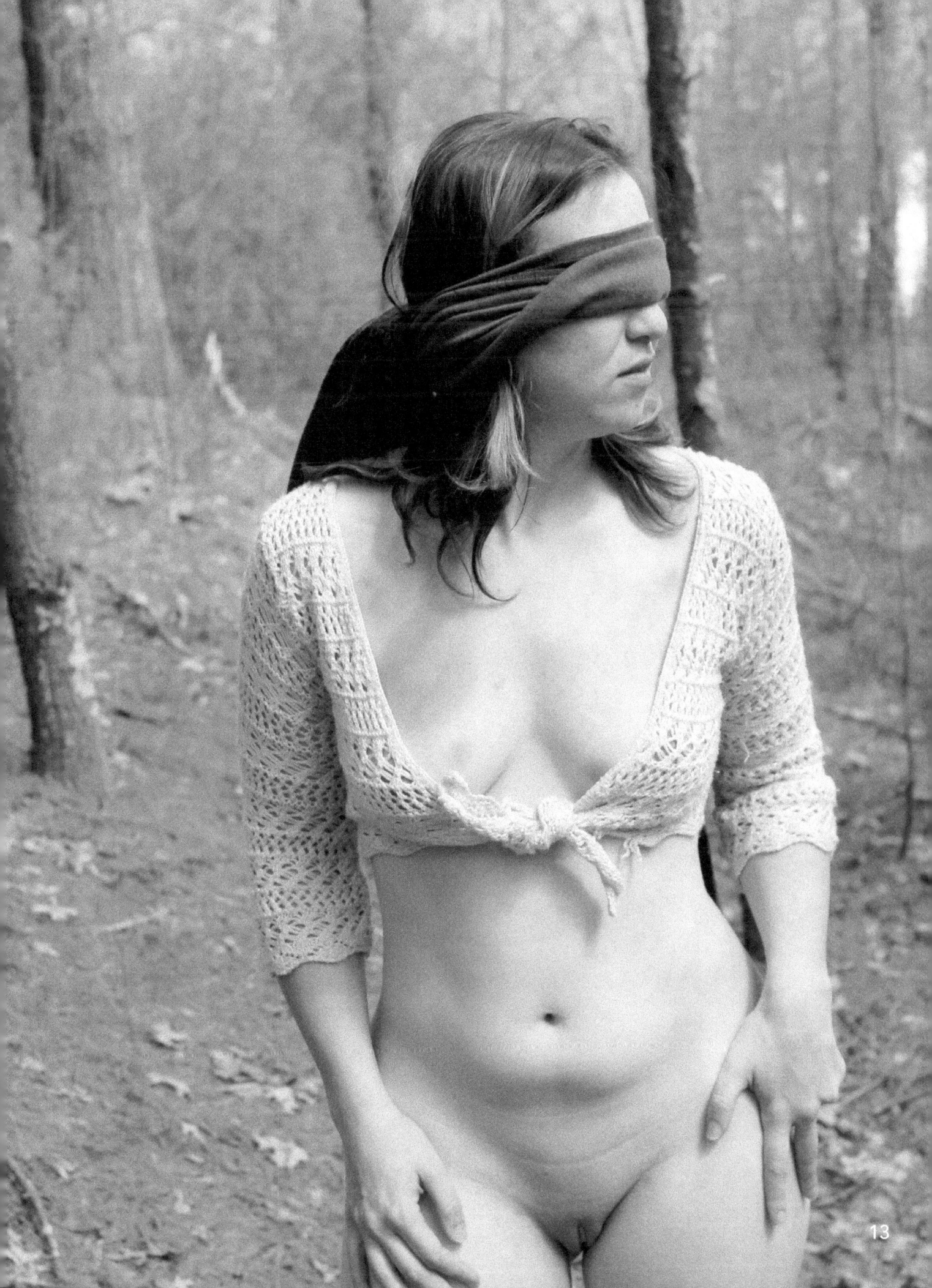

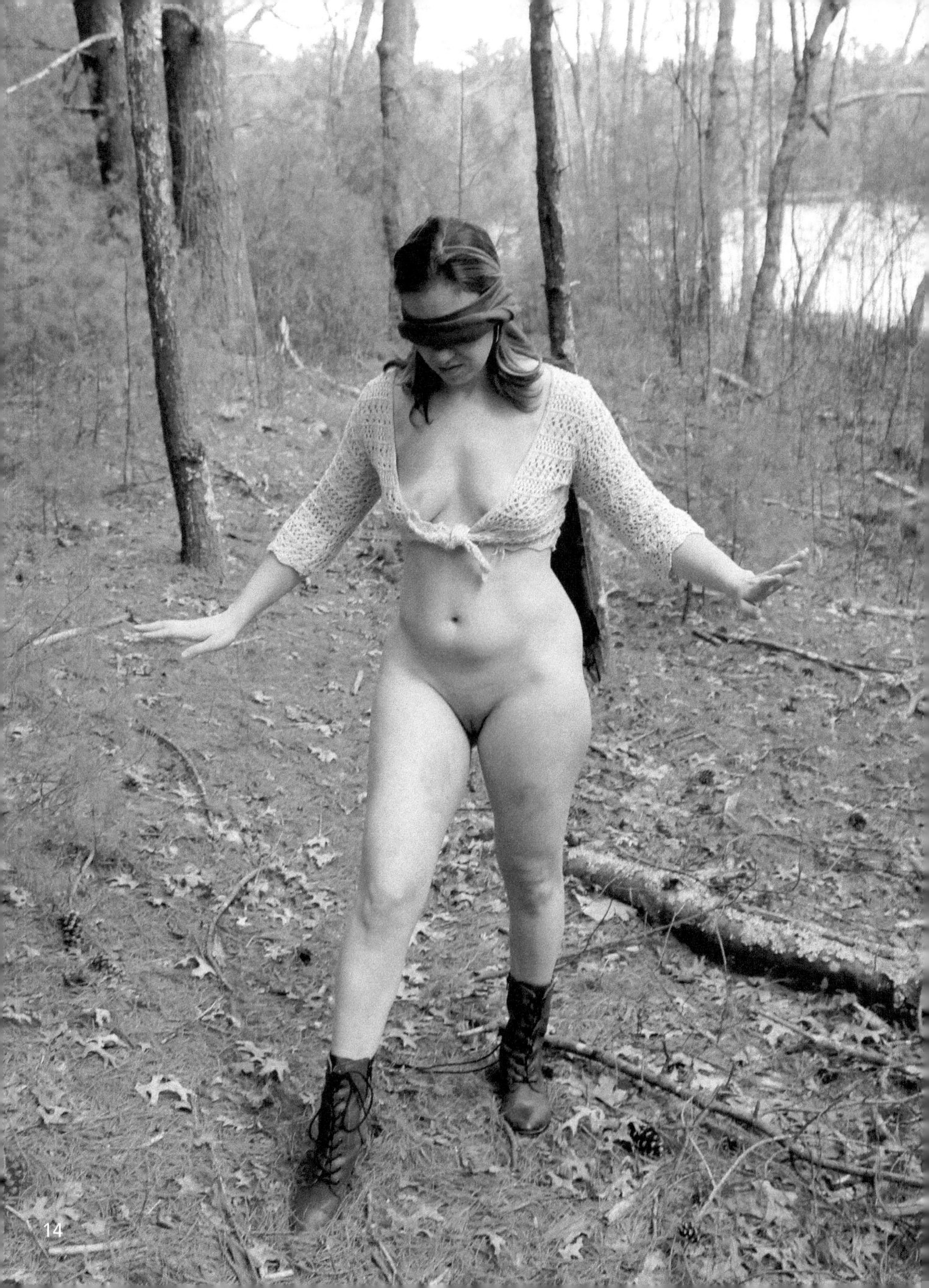

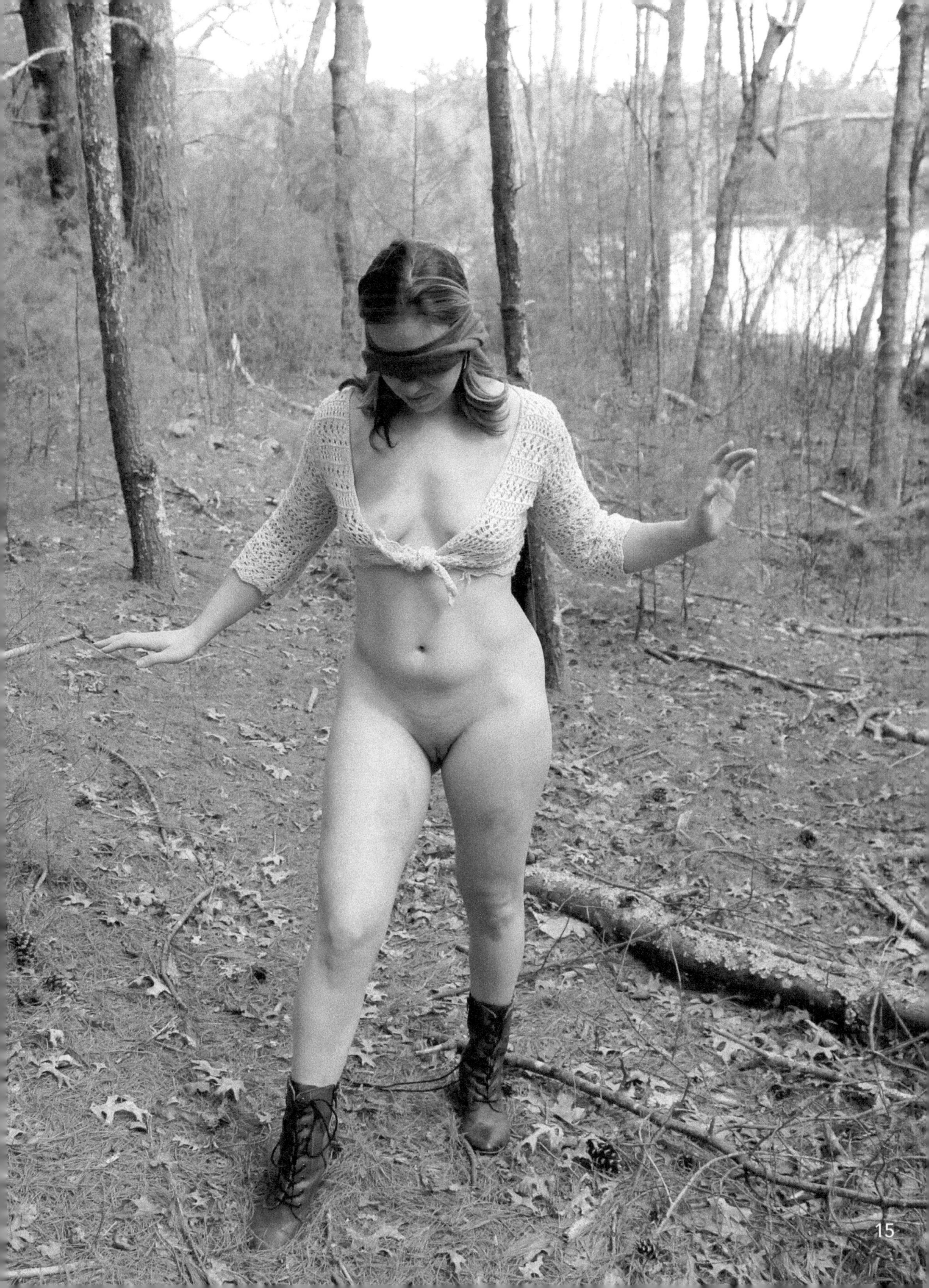

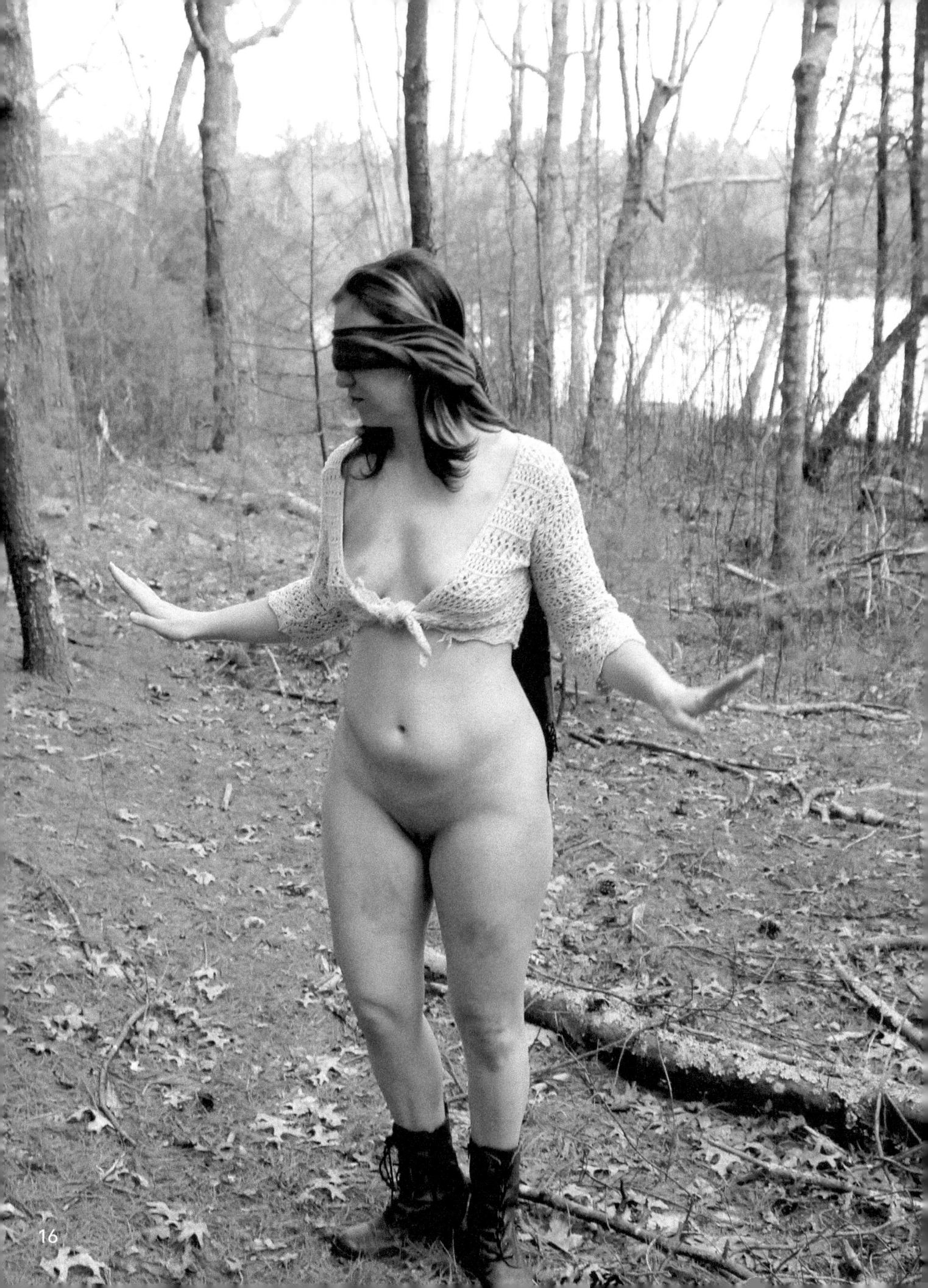

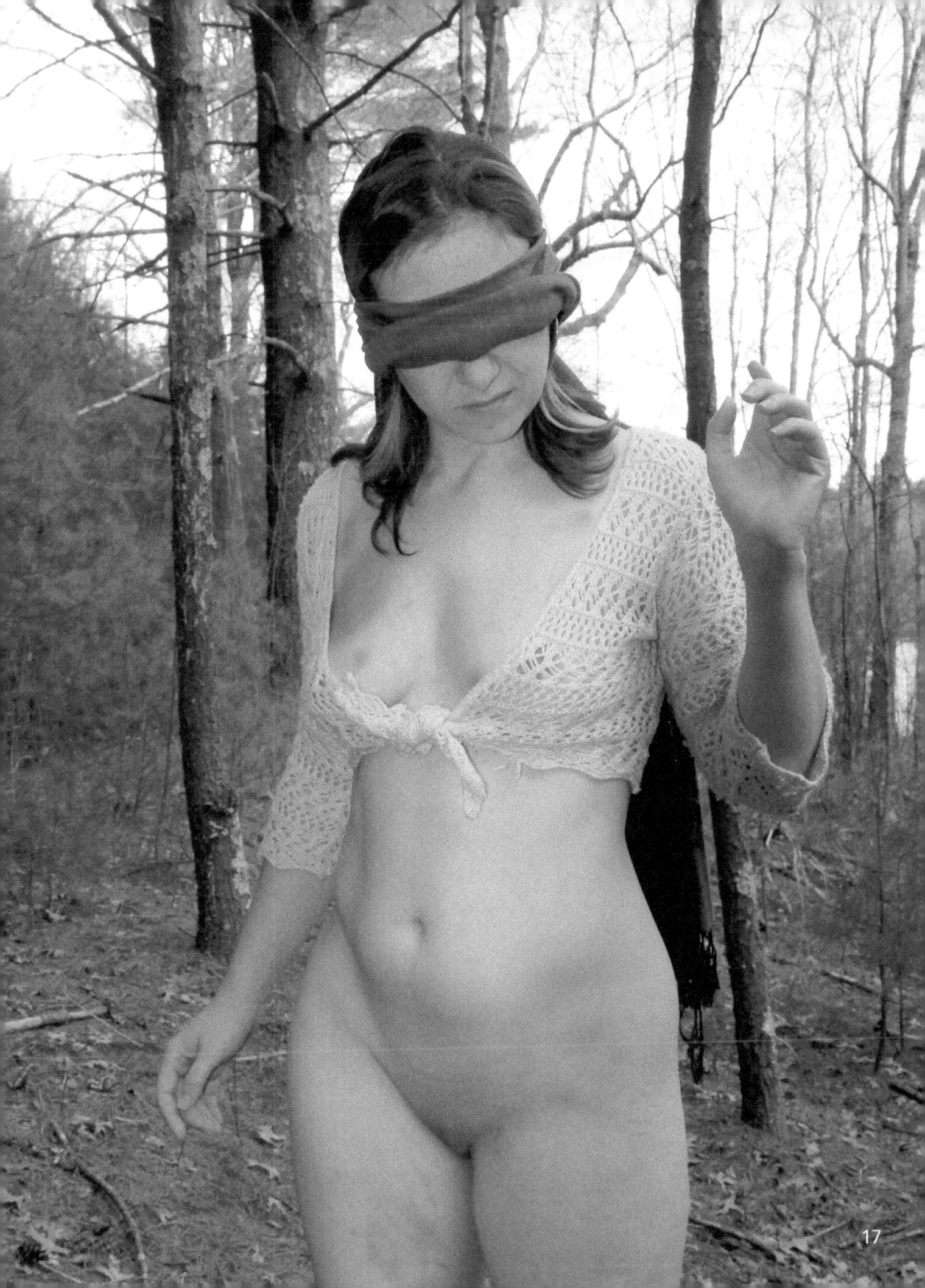

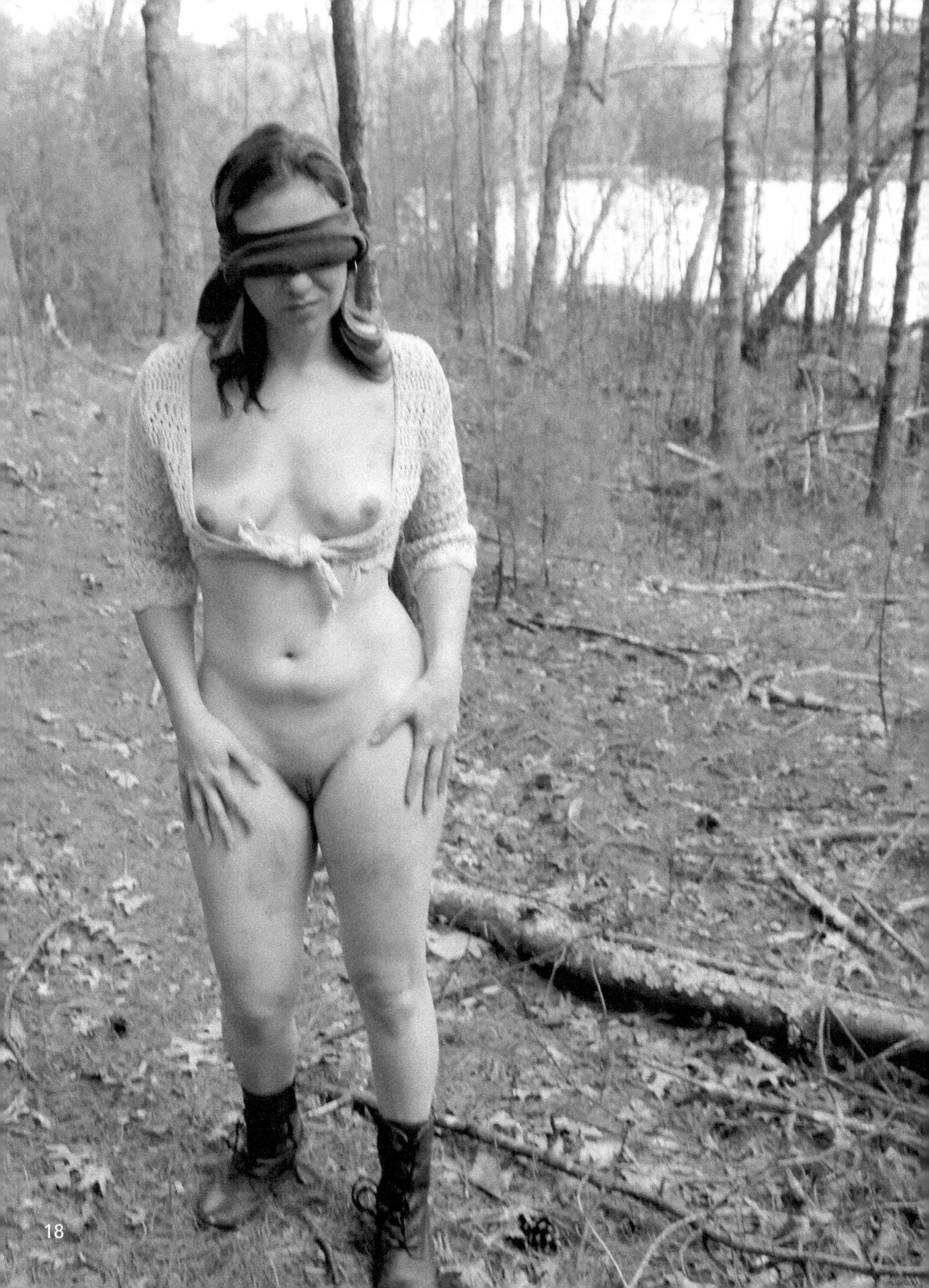

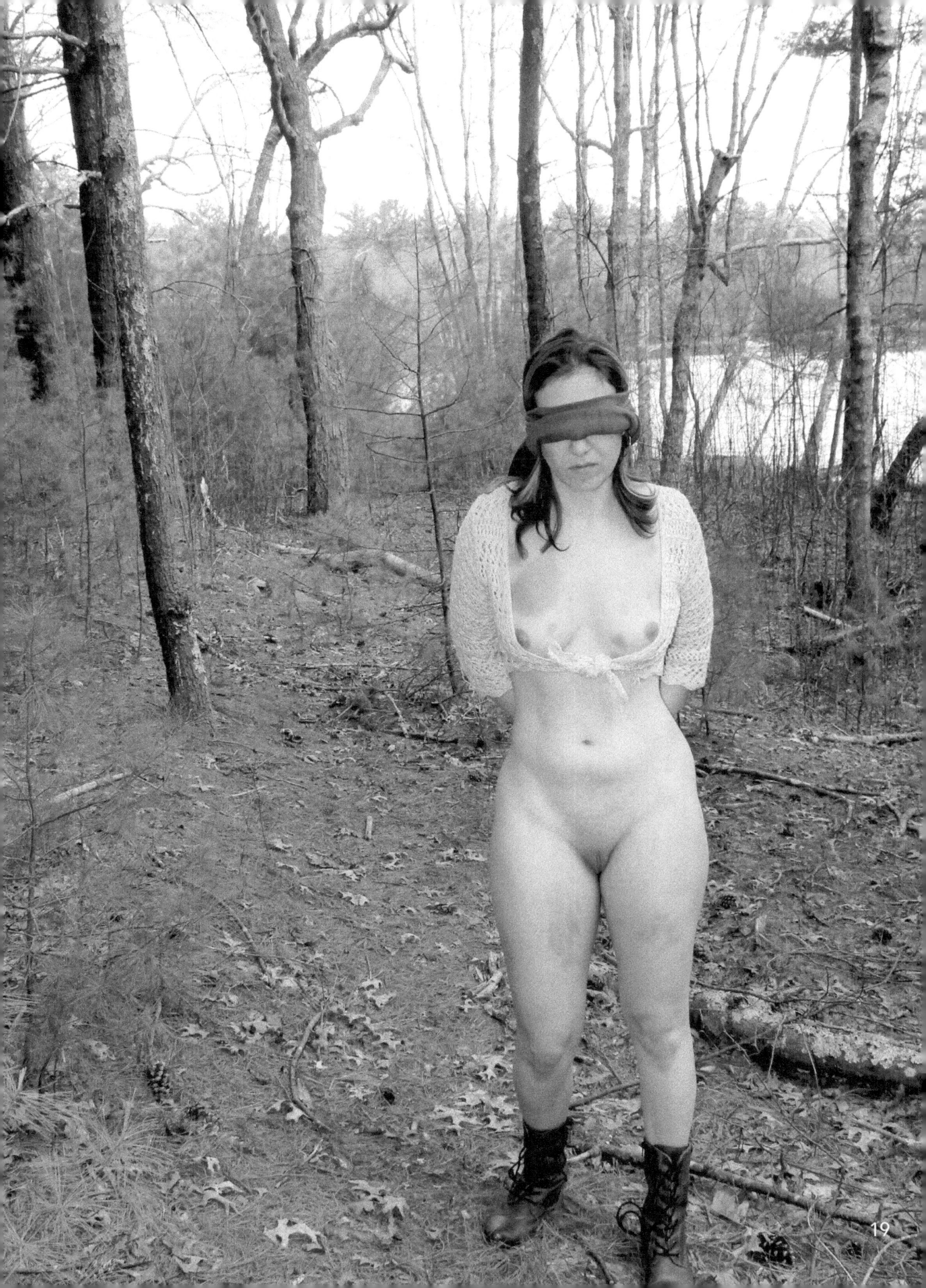

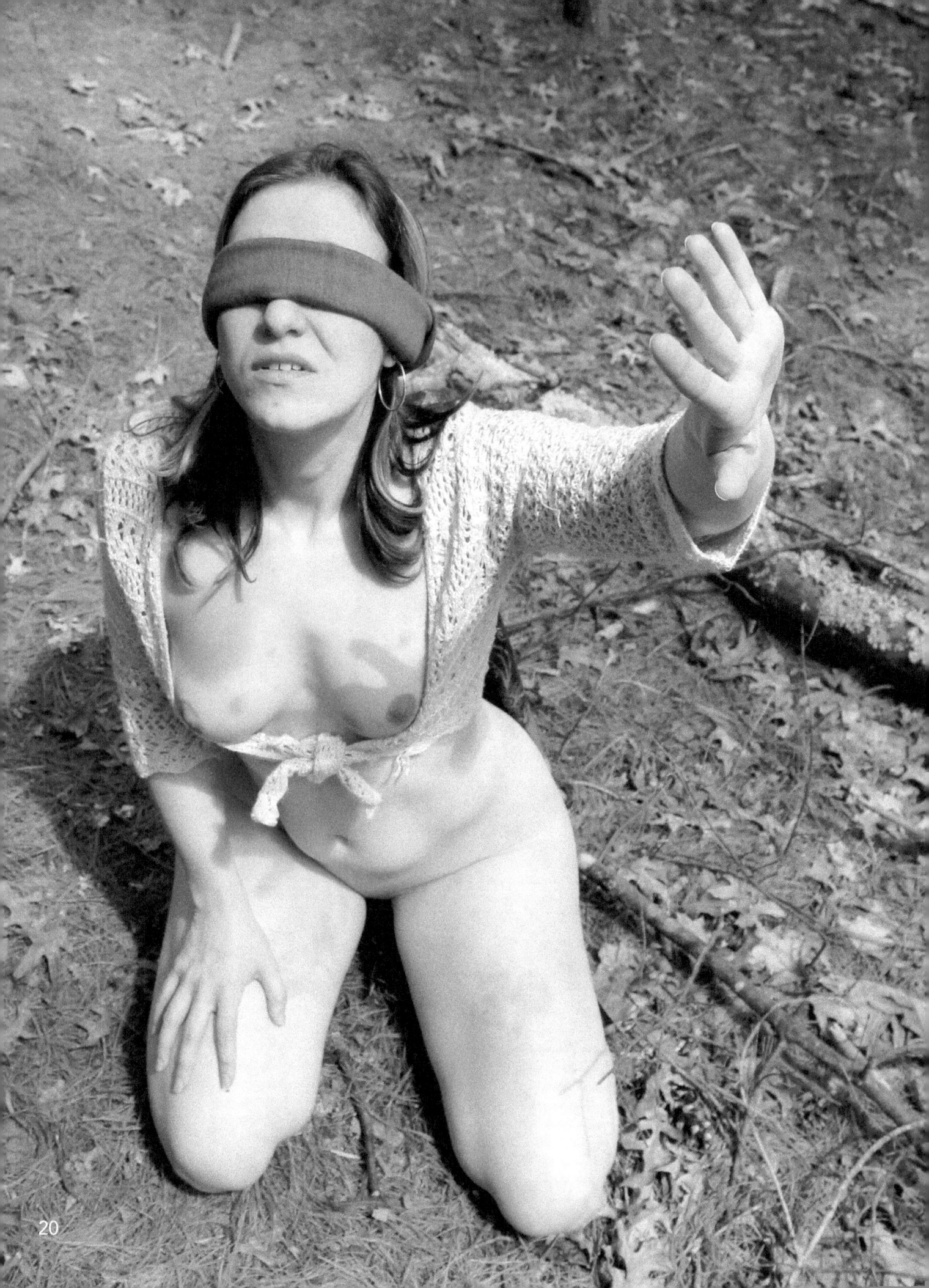

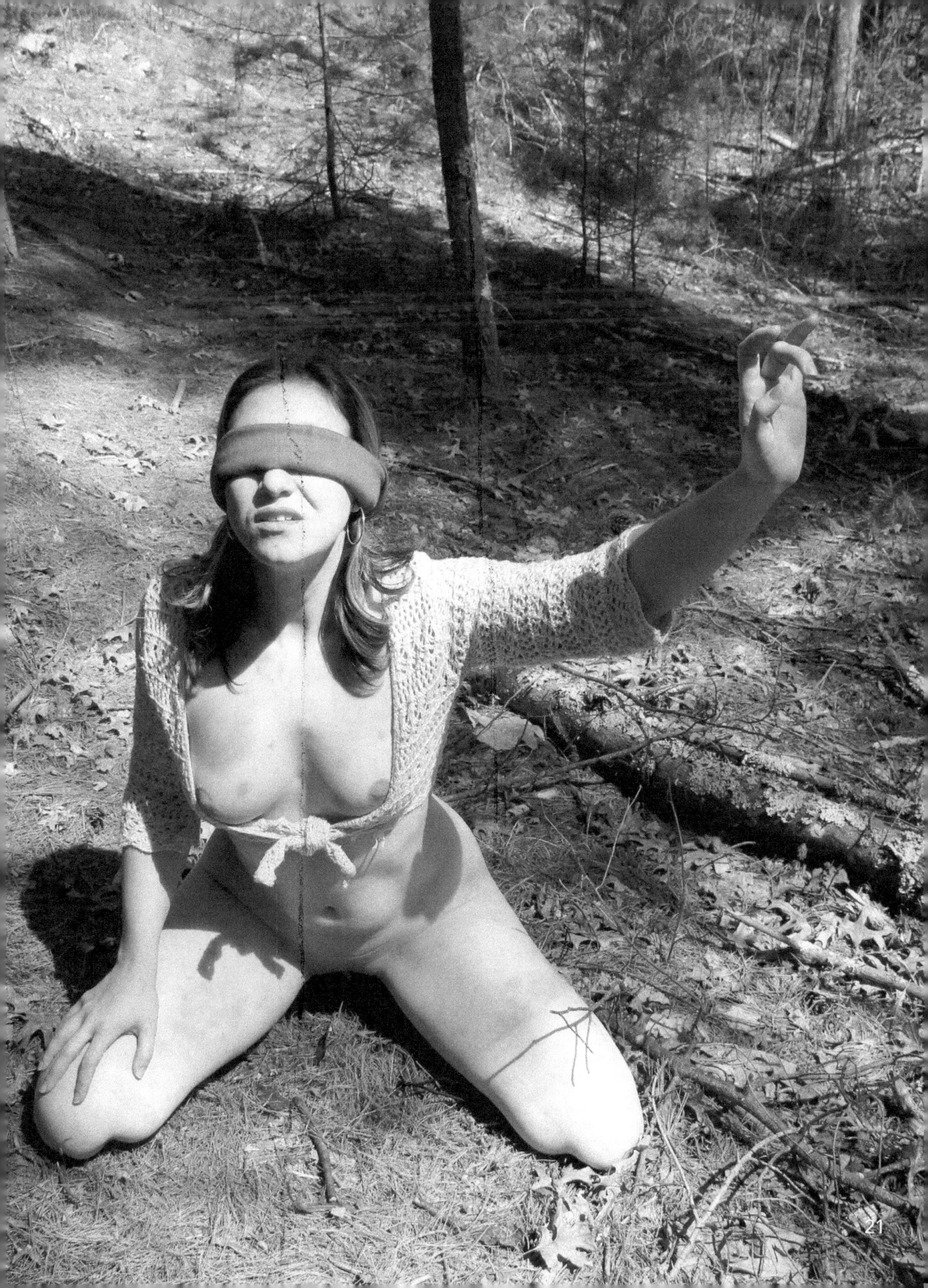

"We're going to depersonalize you in this next set," he says.

"You will need more than a blanket," she stated flatly

Three

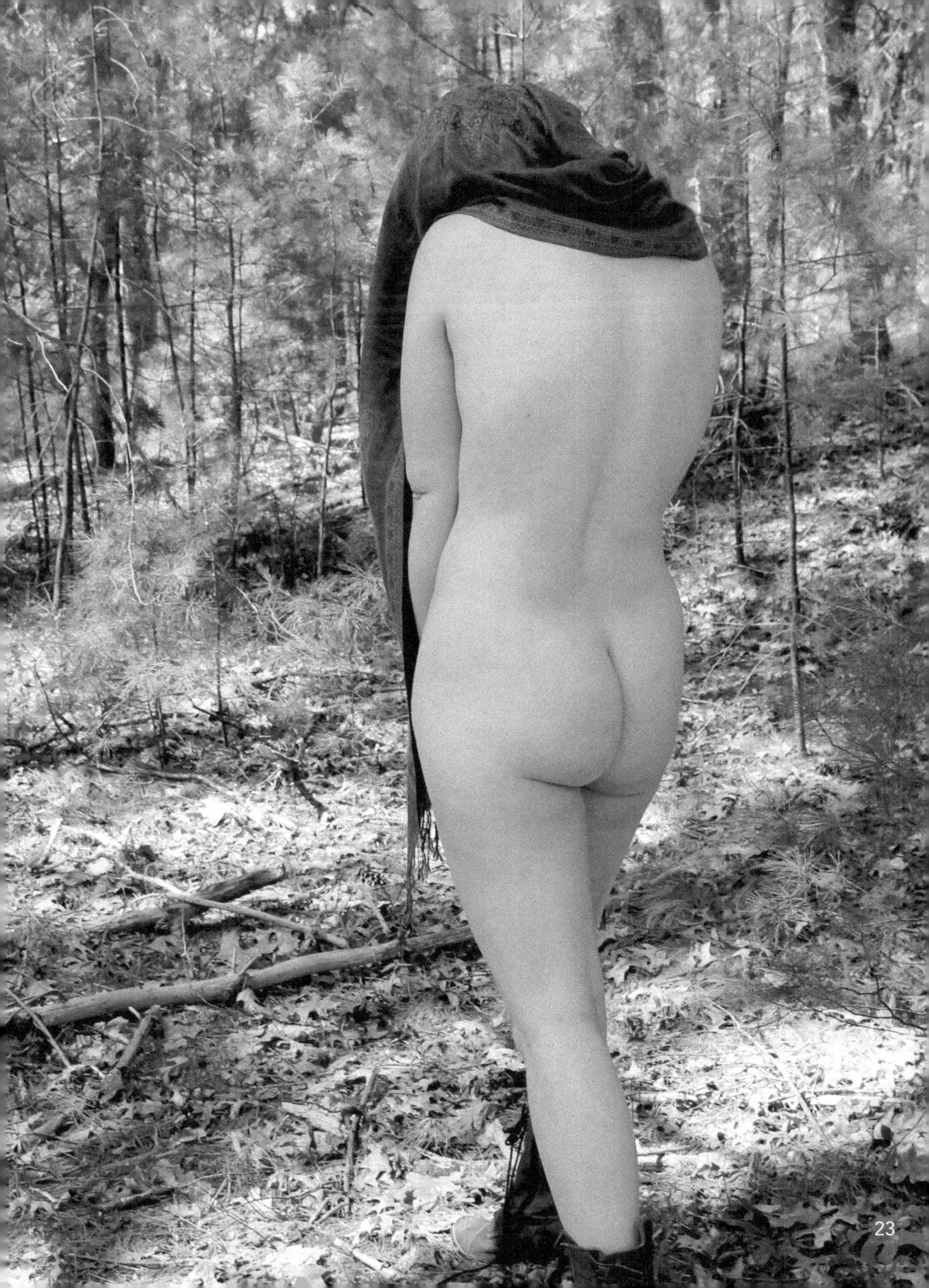

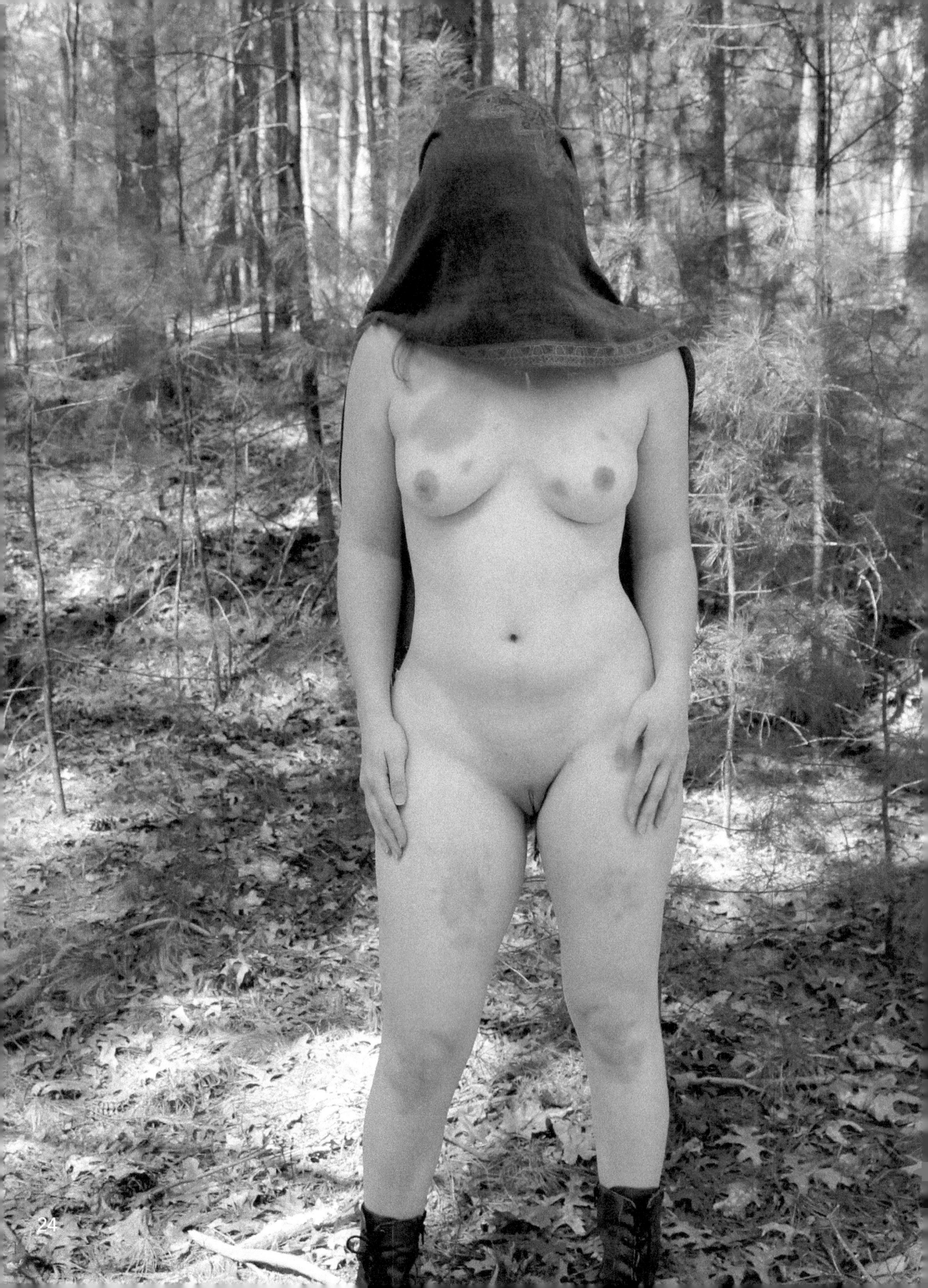

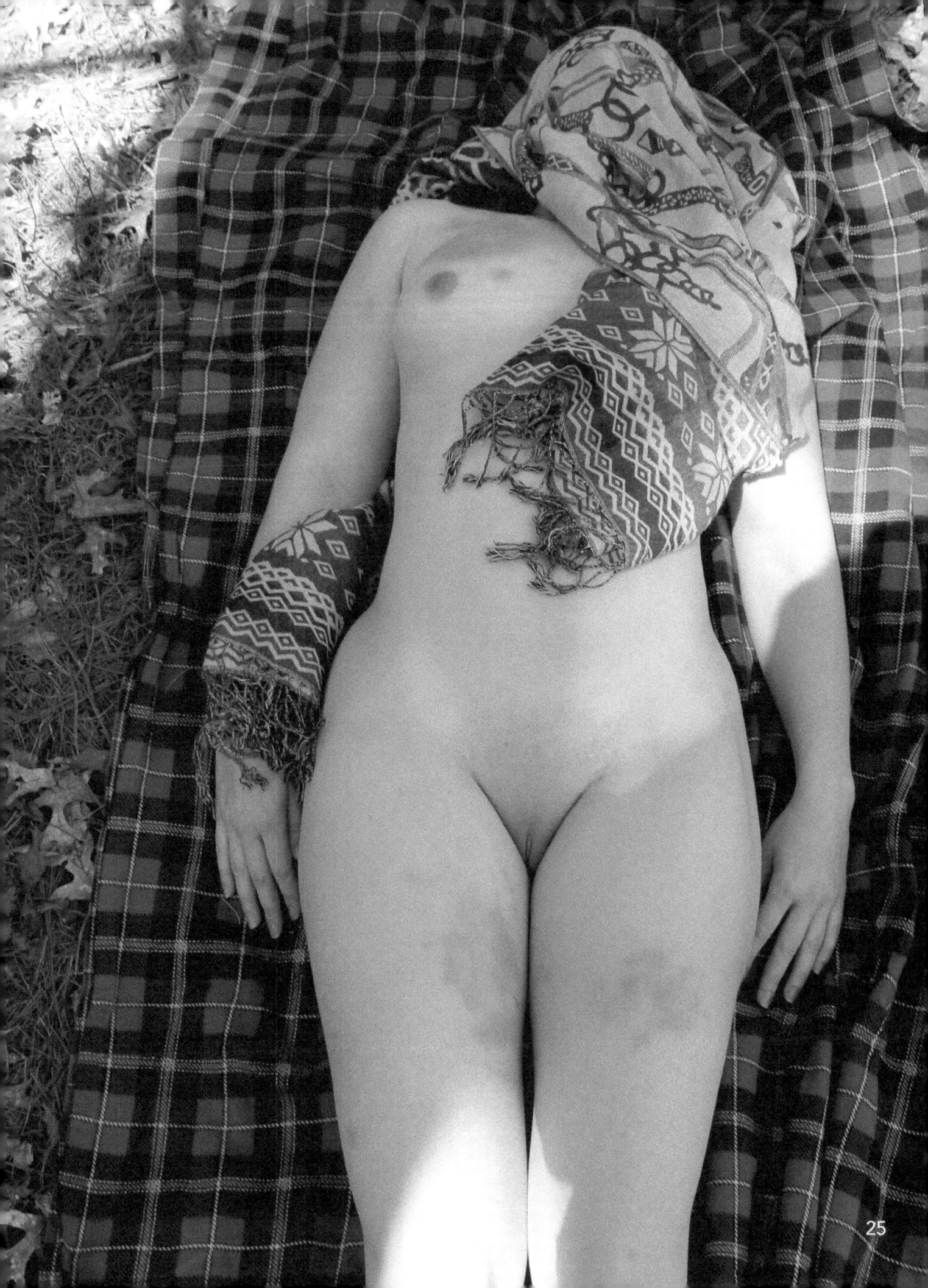

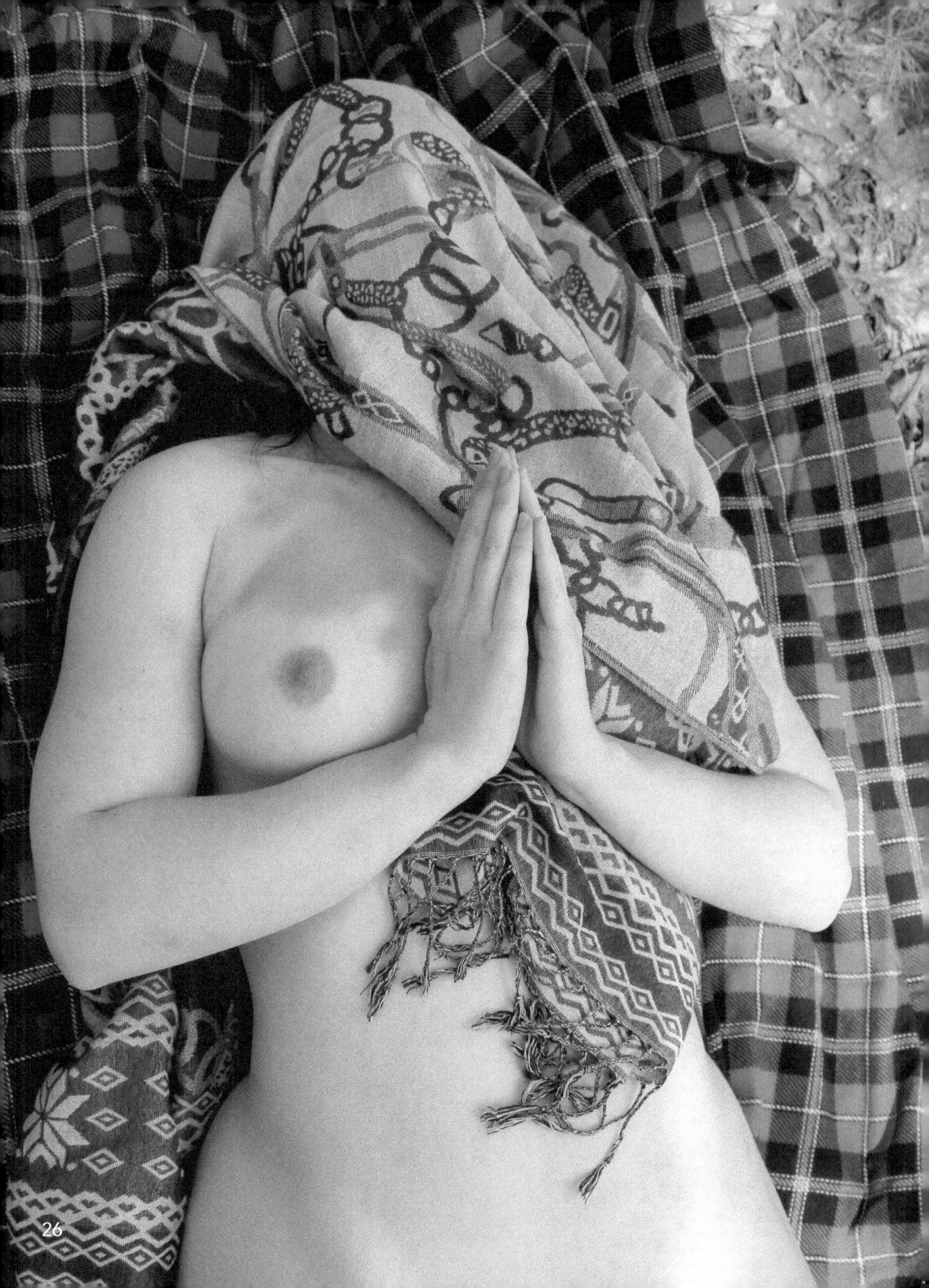

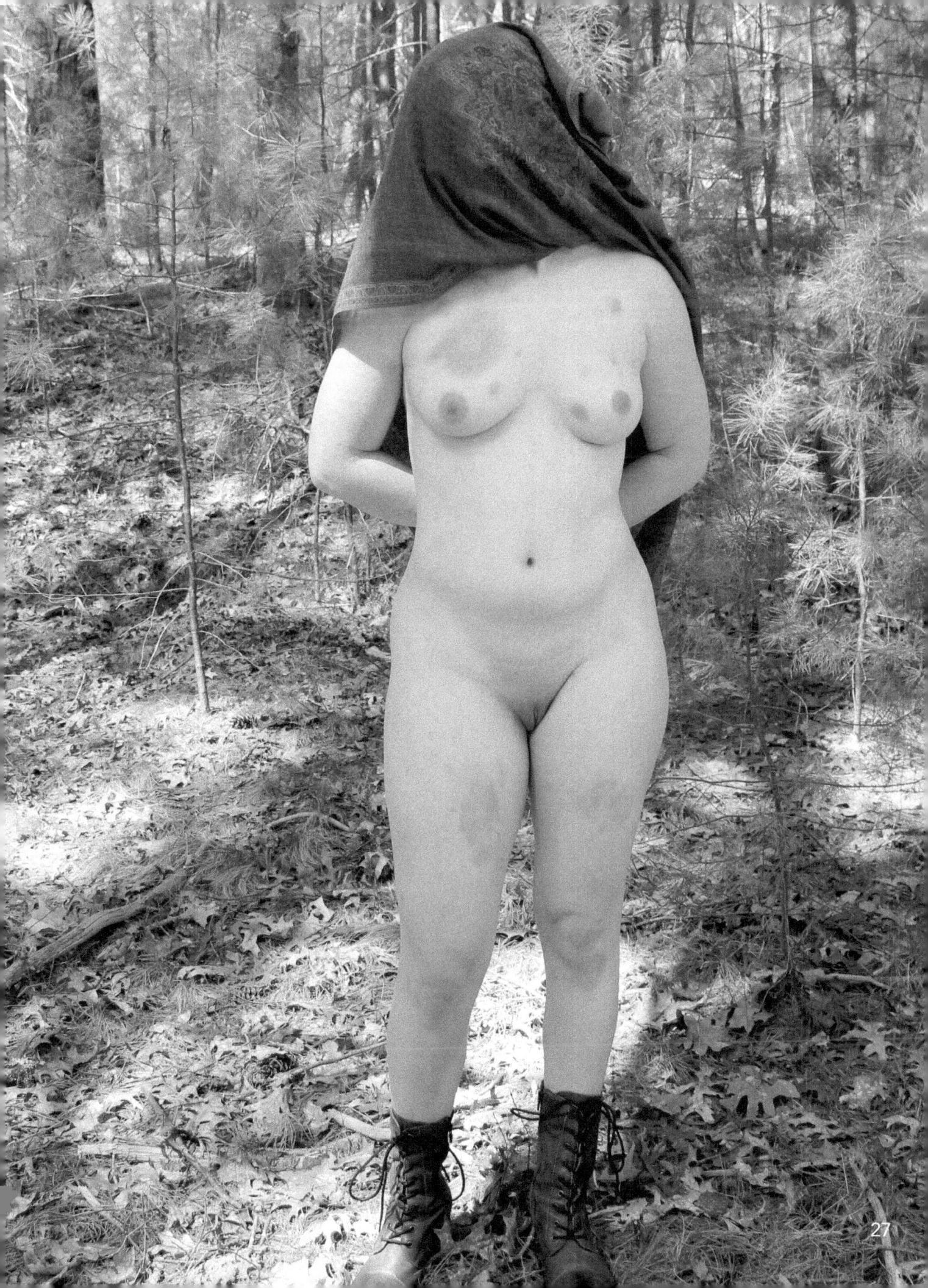

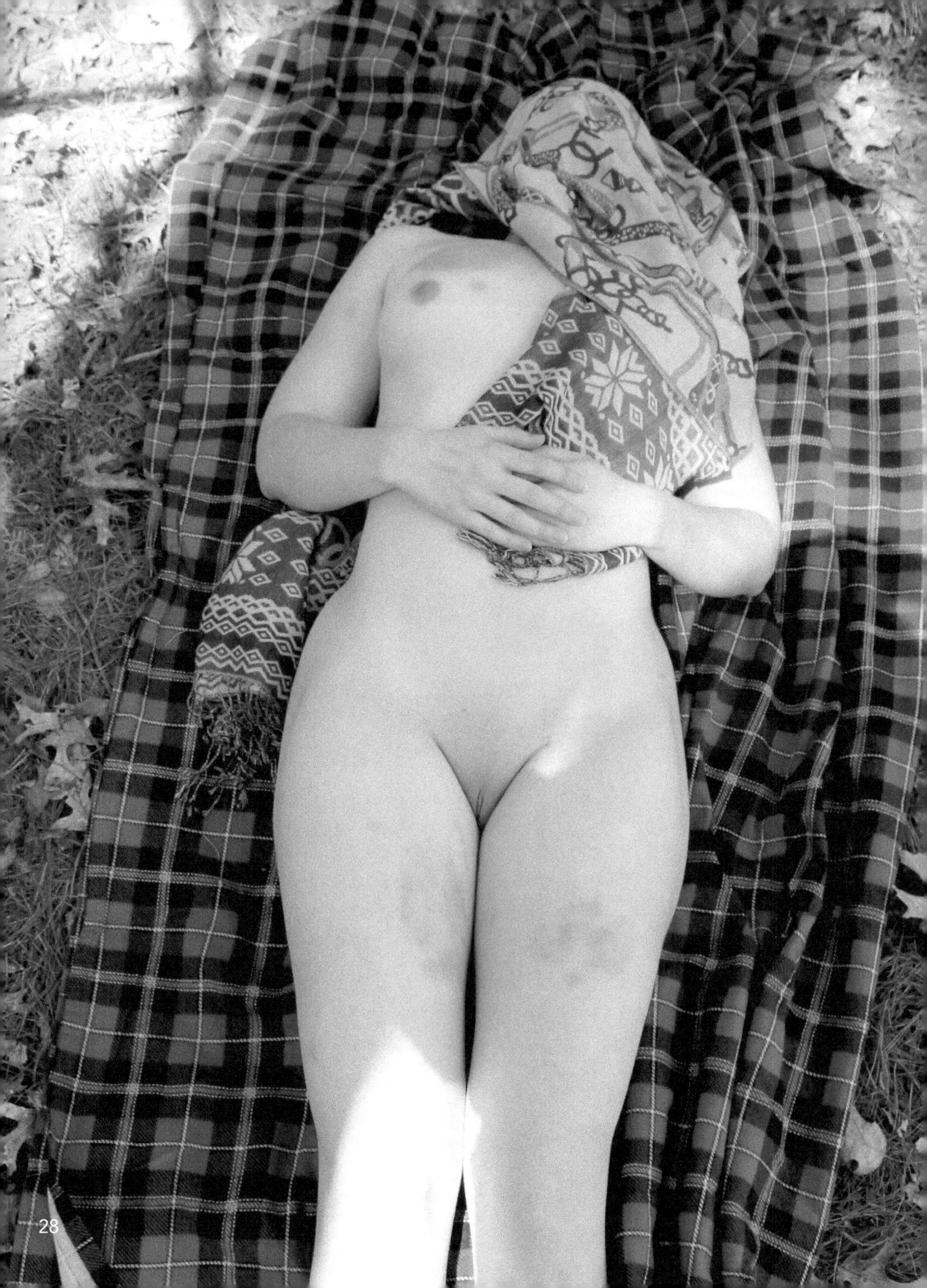

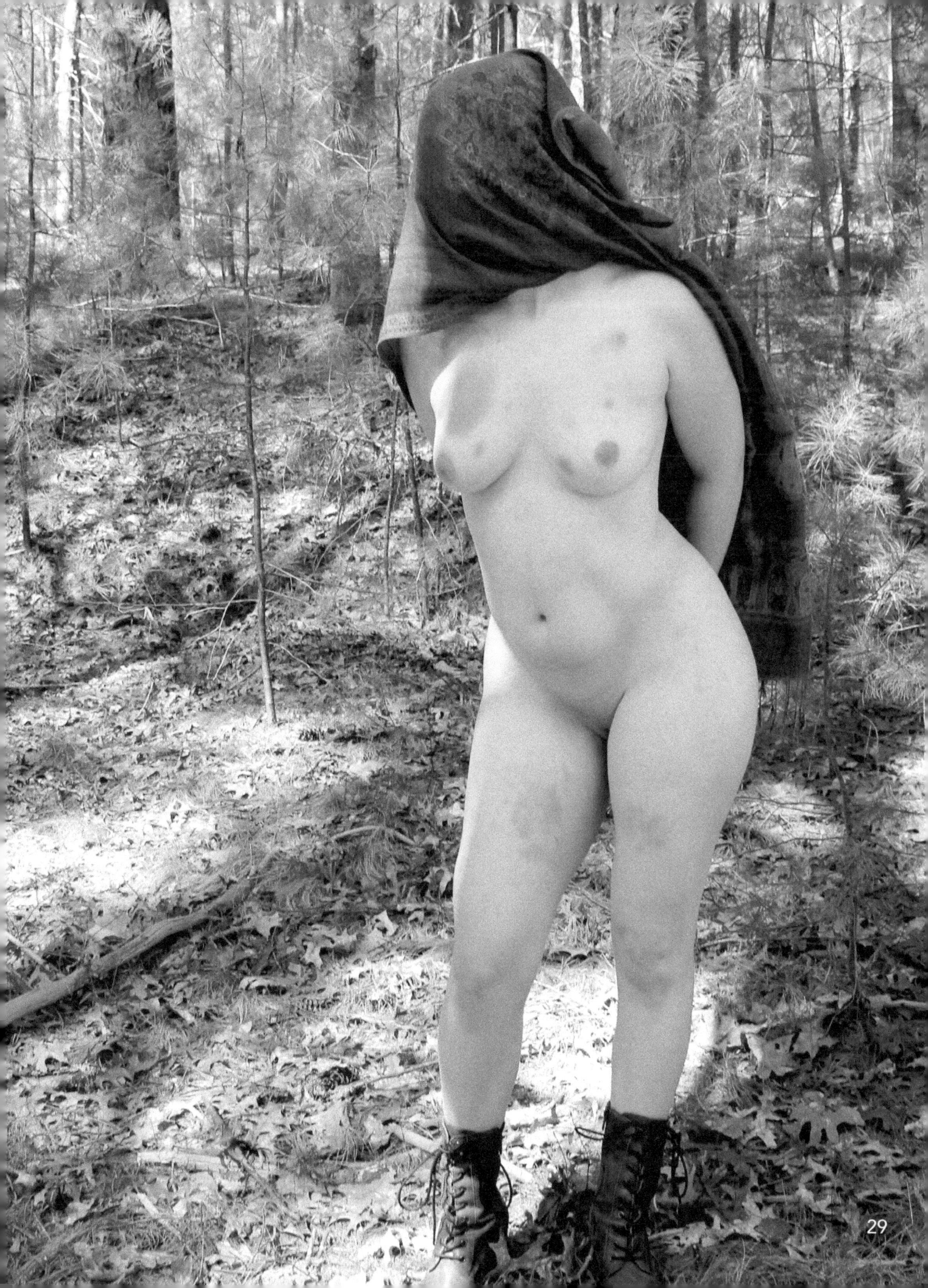

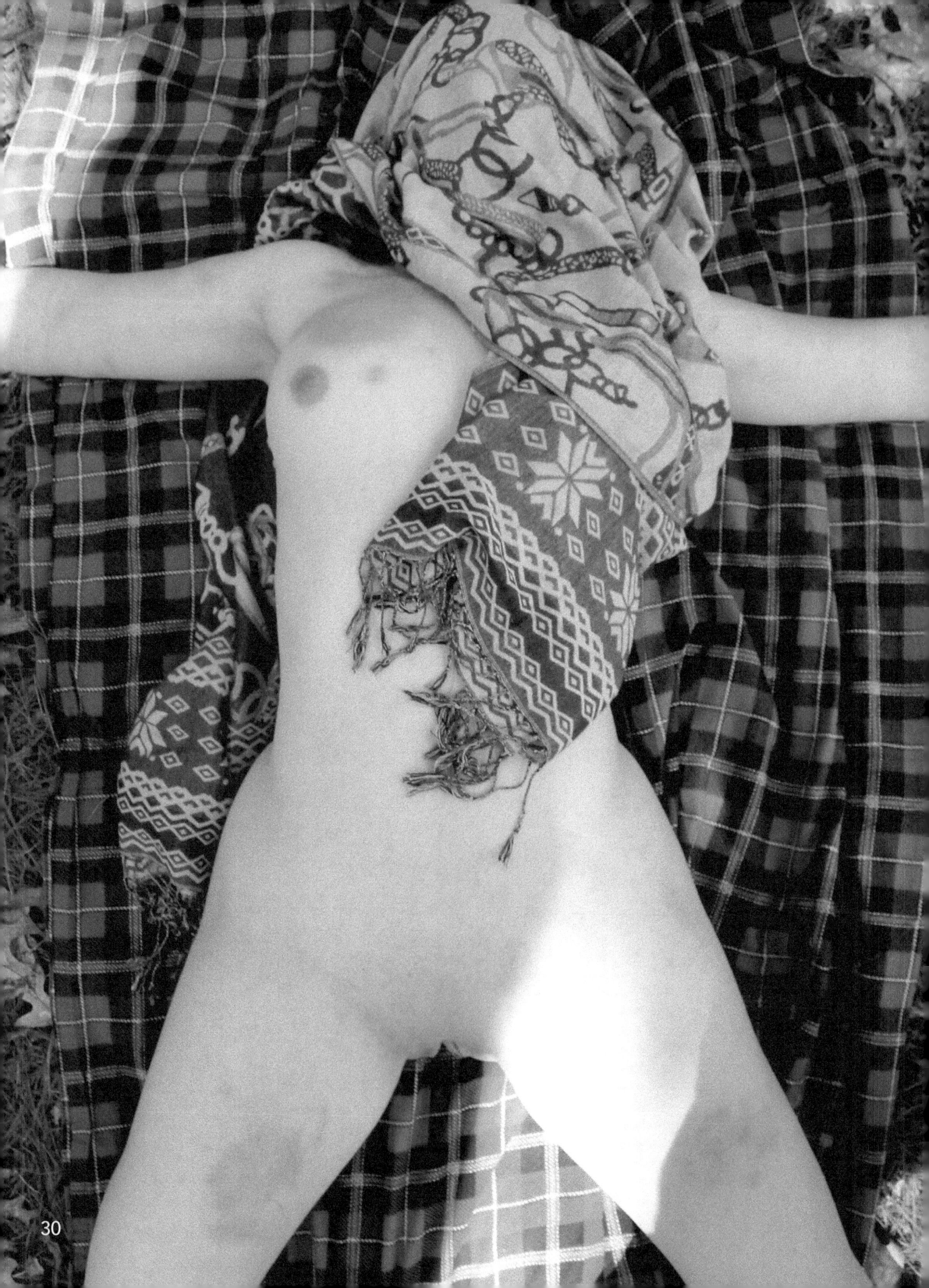

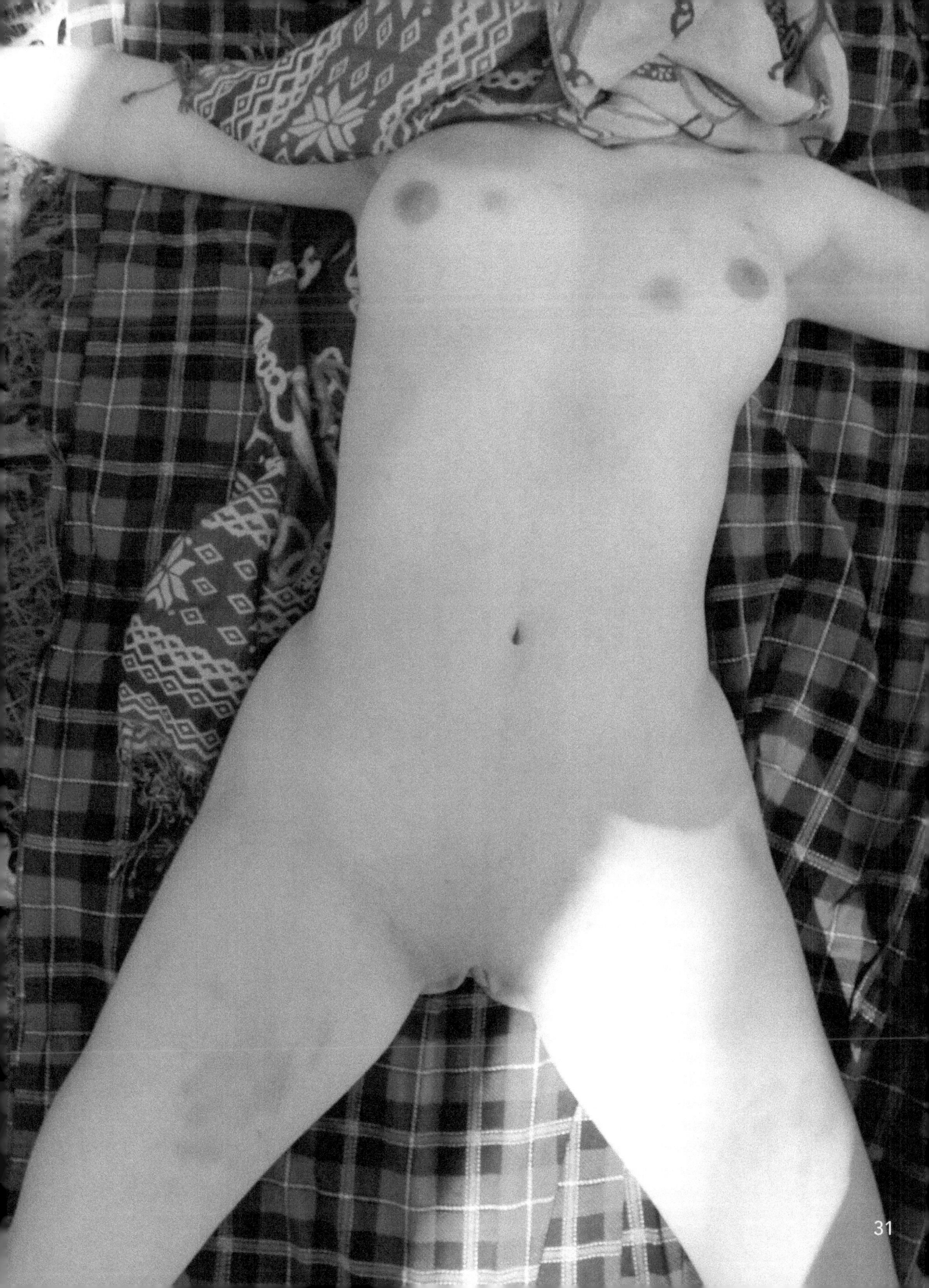

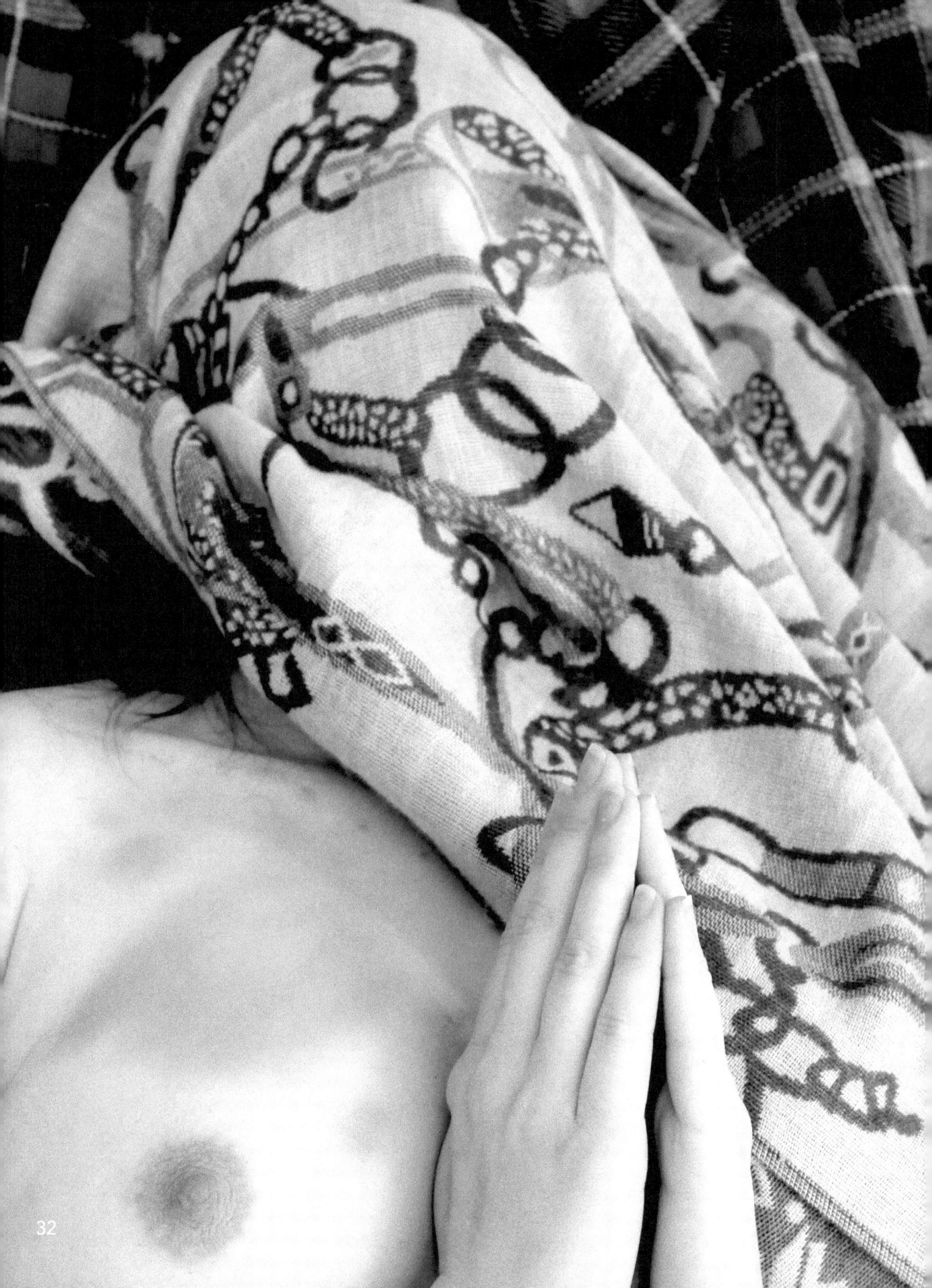

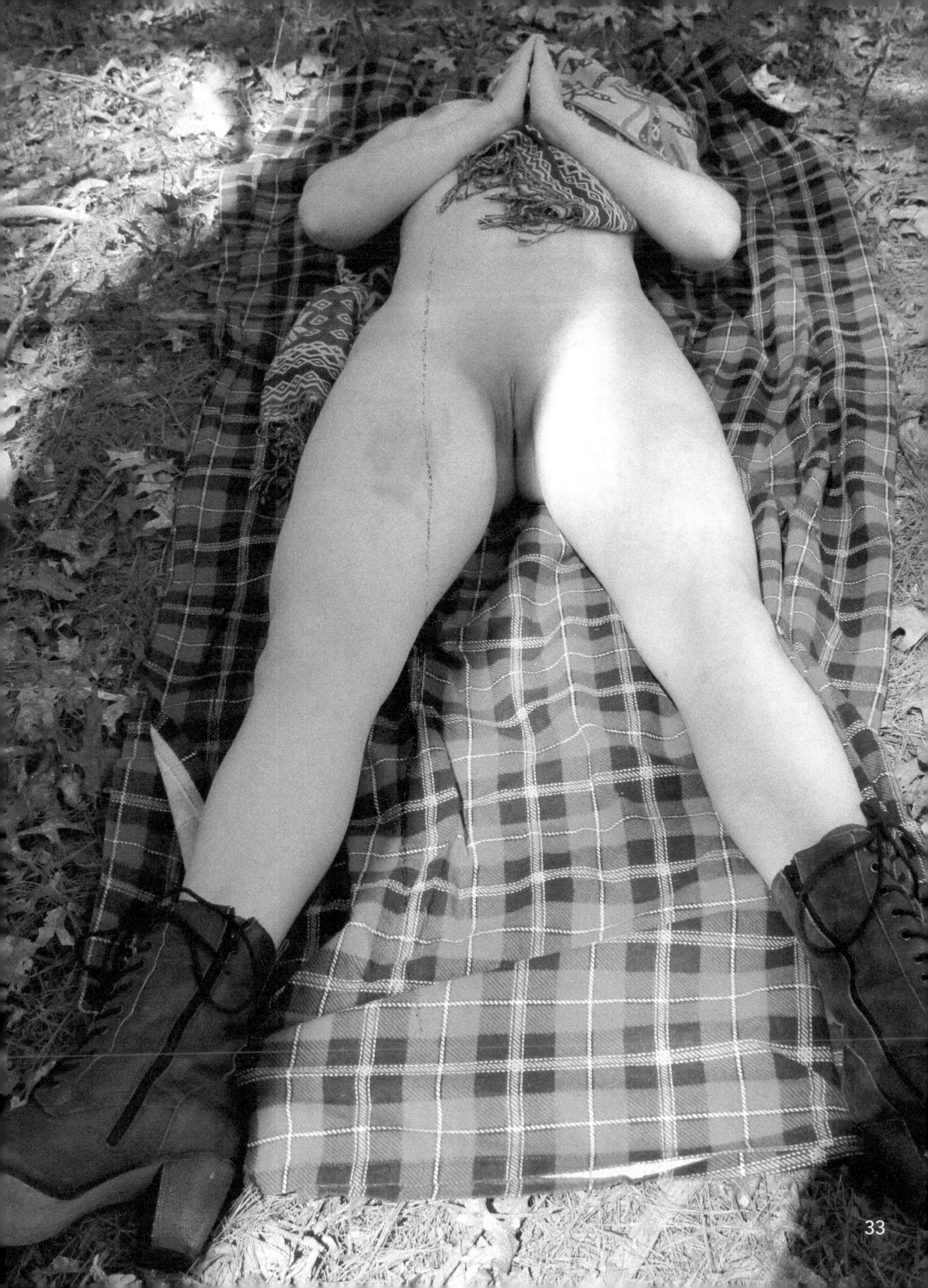

"Can you play dead?" he asks.

"Sure!" she says, "I used to wish I was often enough."

"We're going to get a little weird."

Macabre, indeed

Four

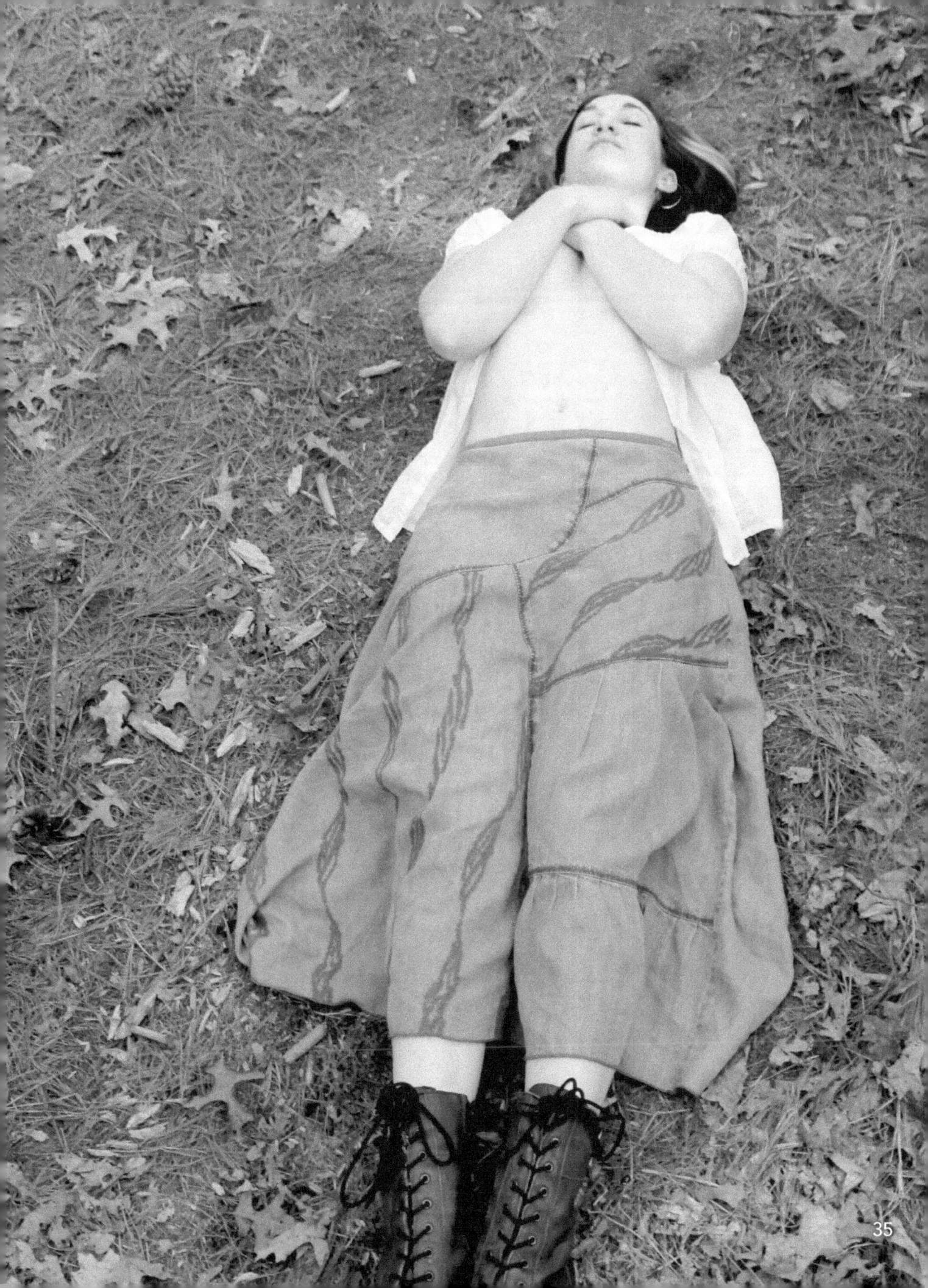

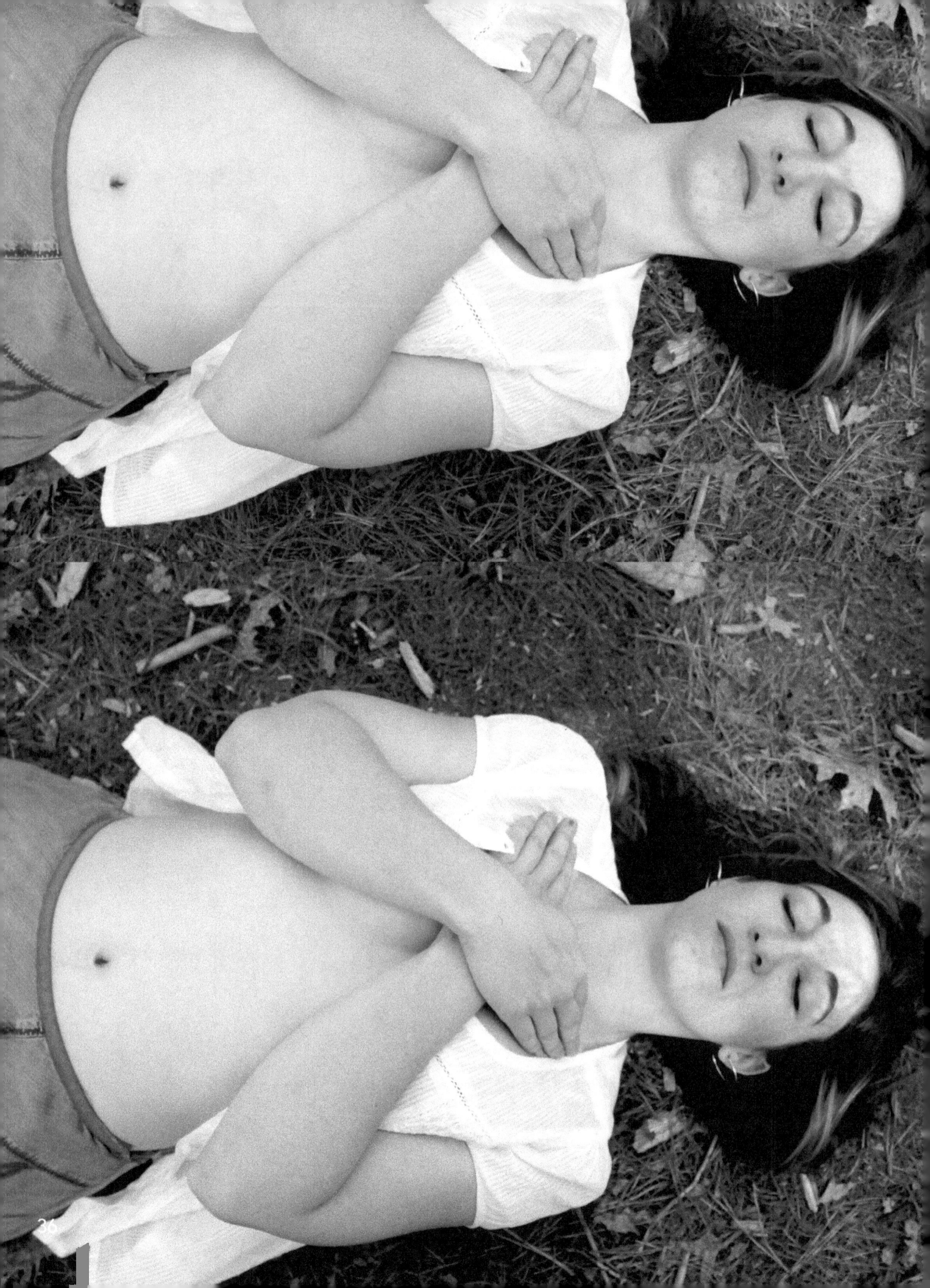

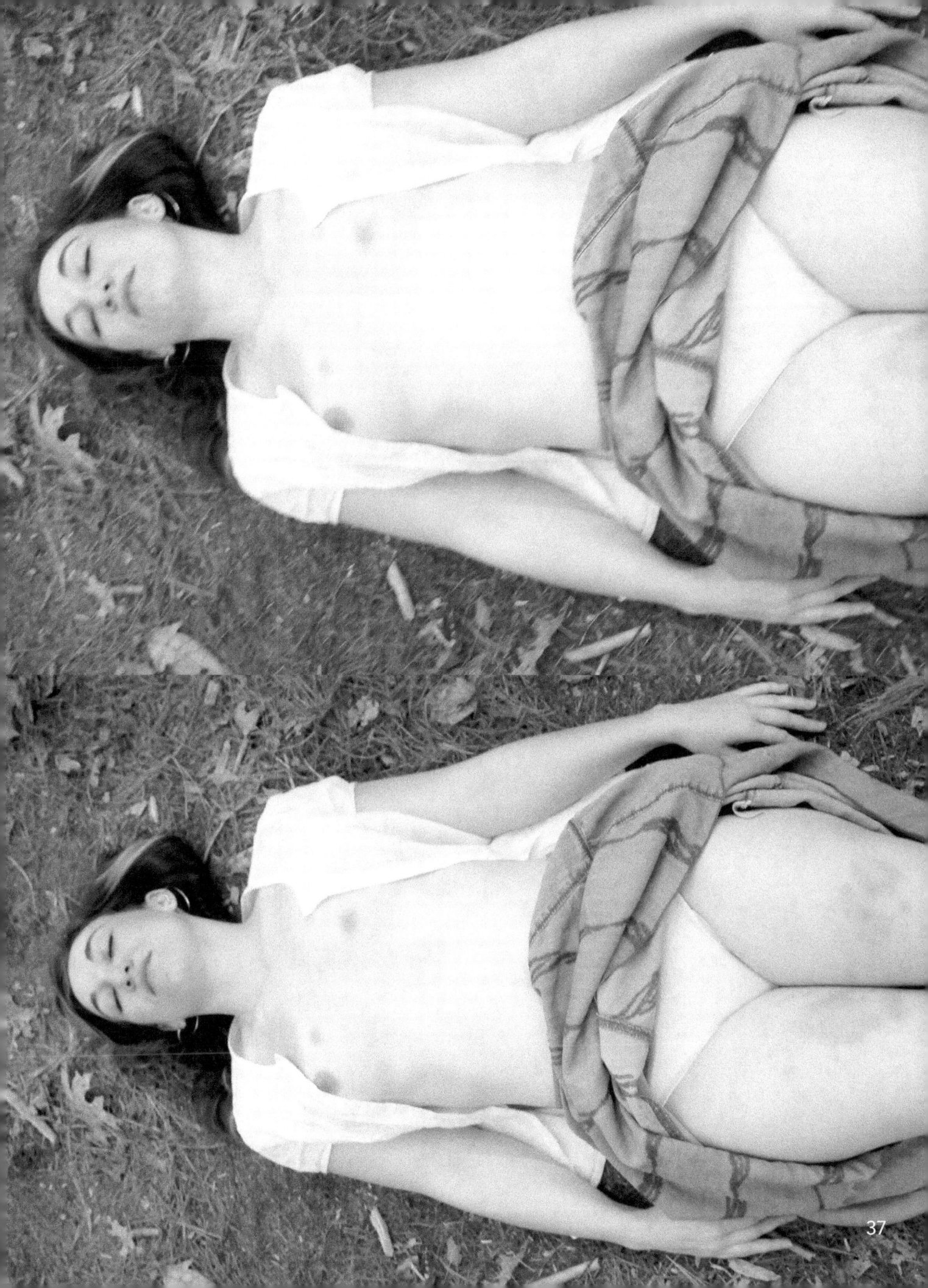

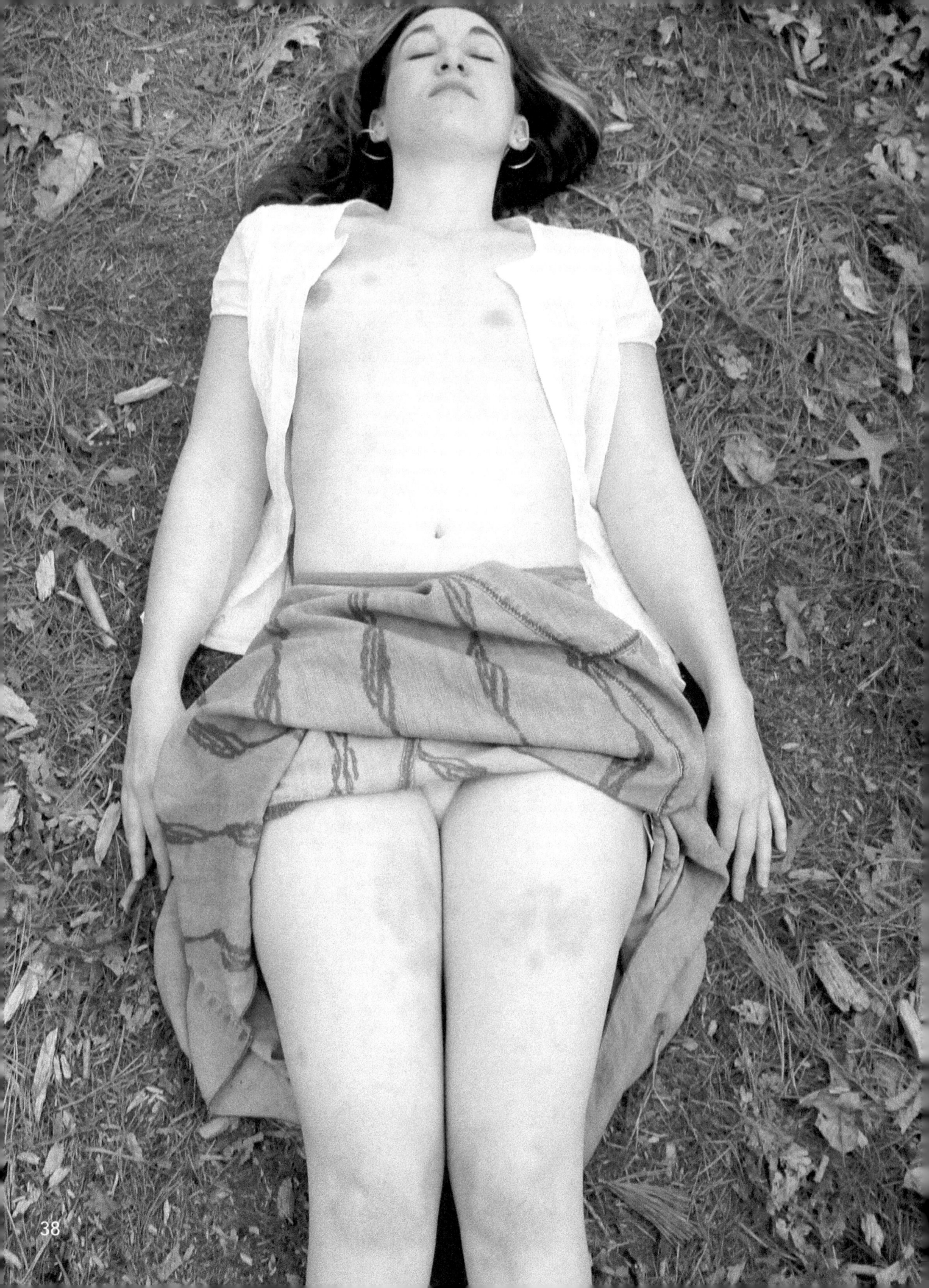

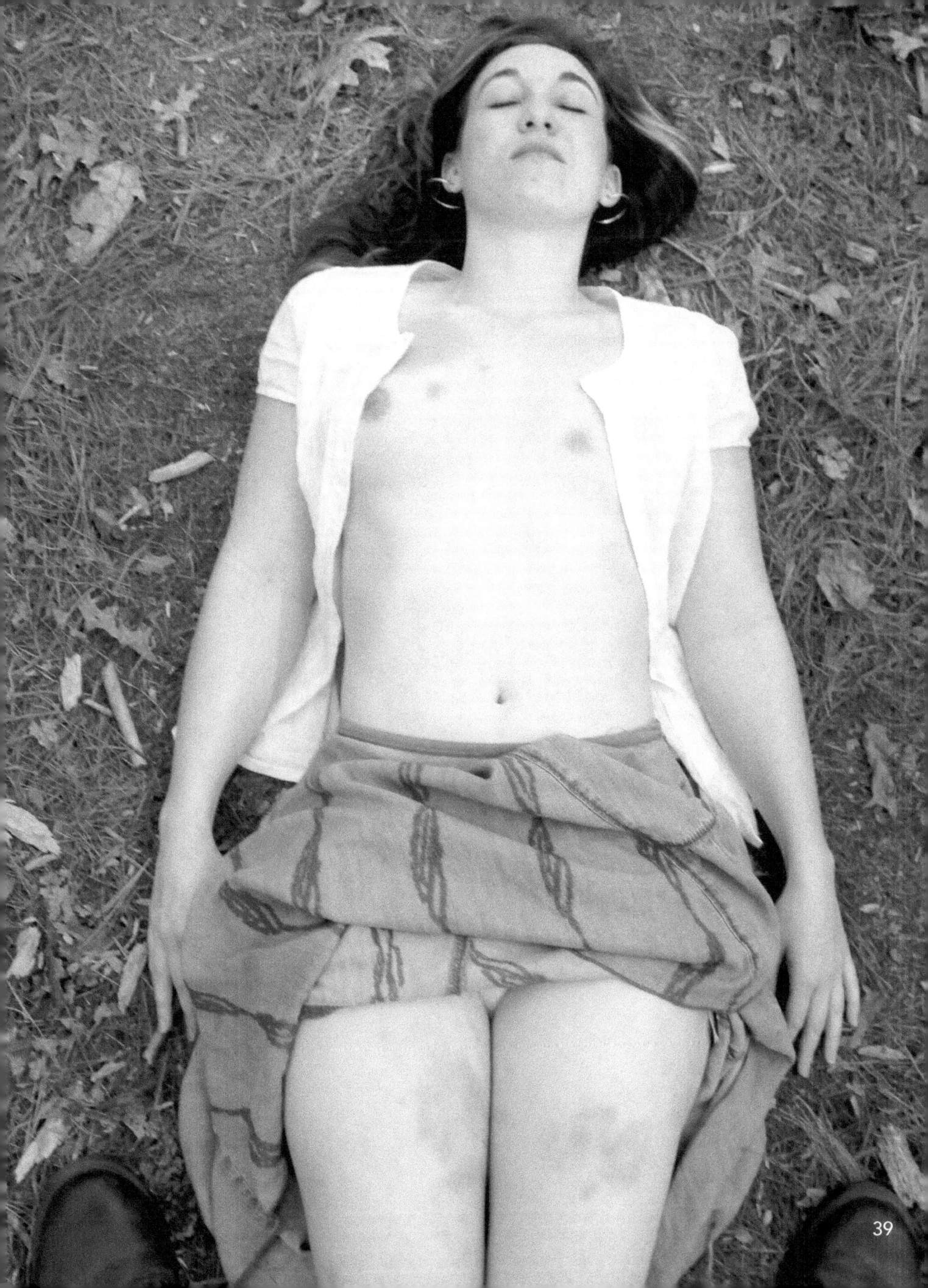

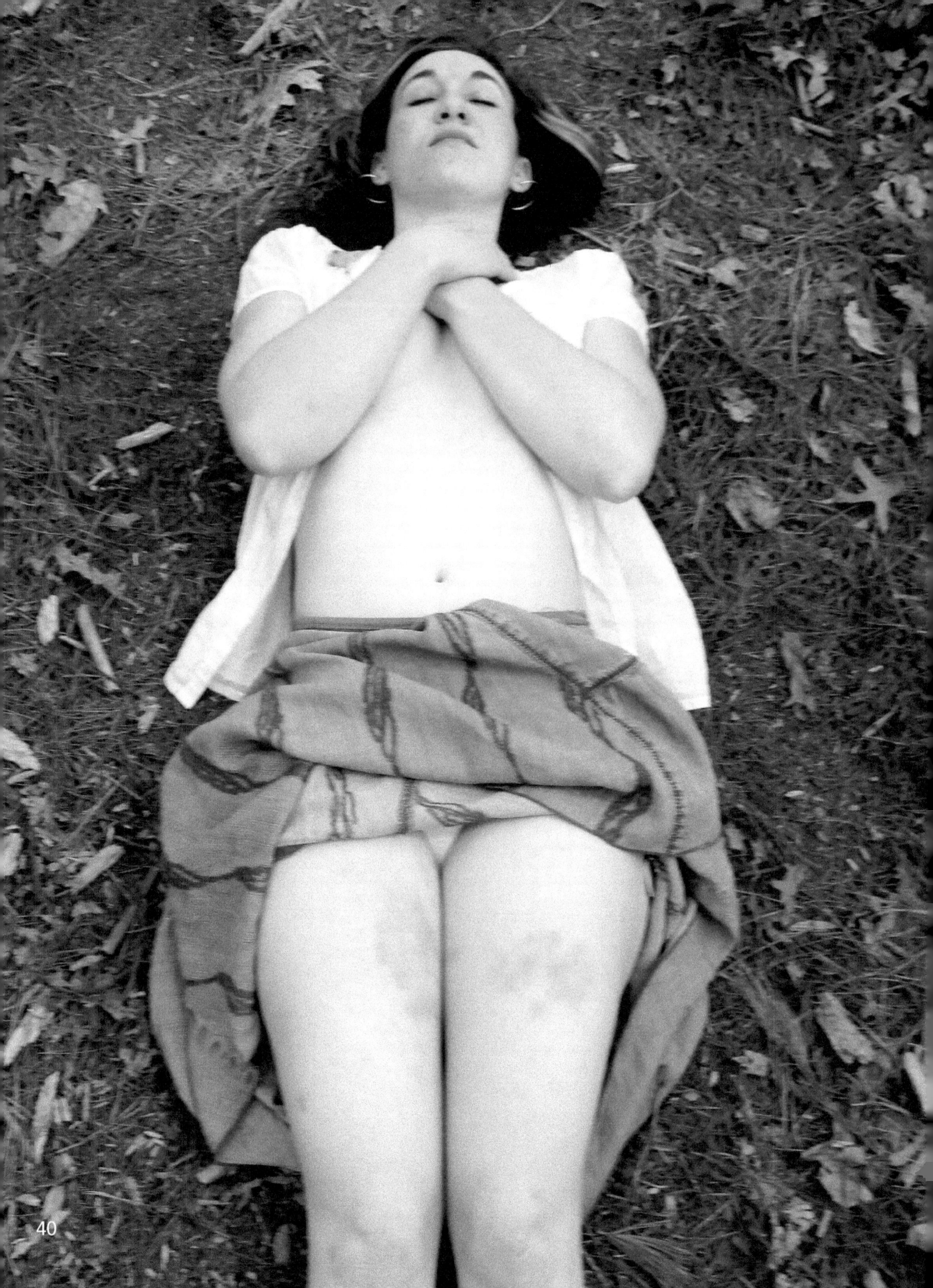

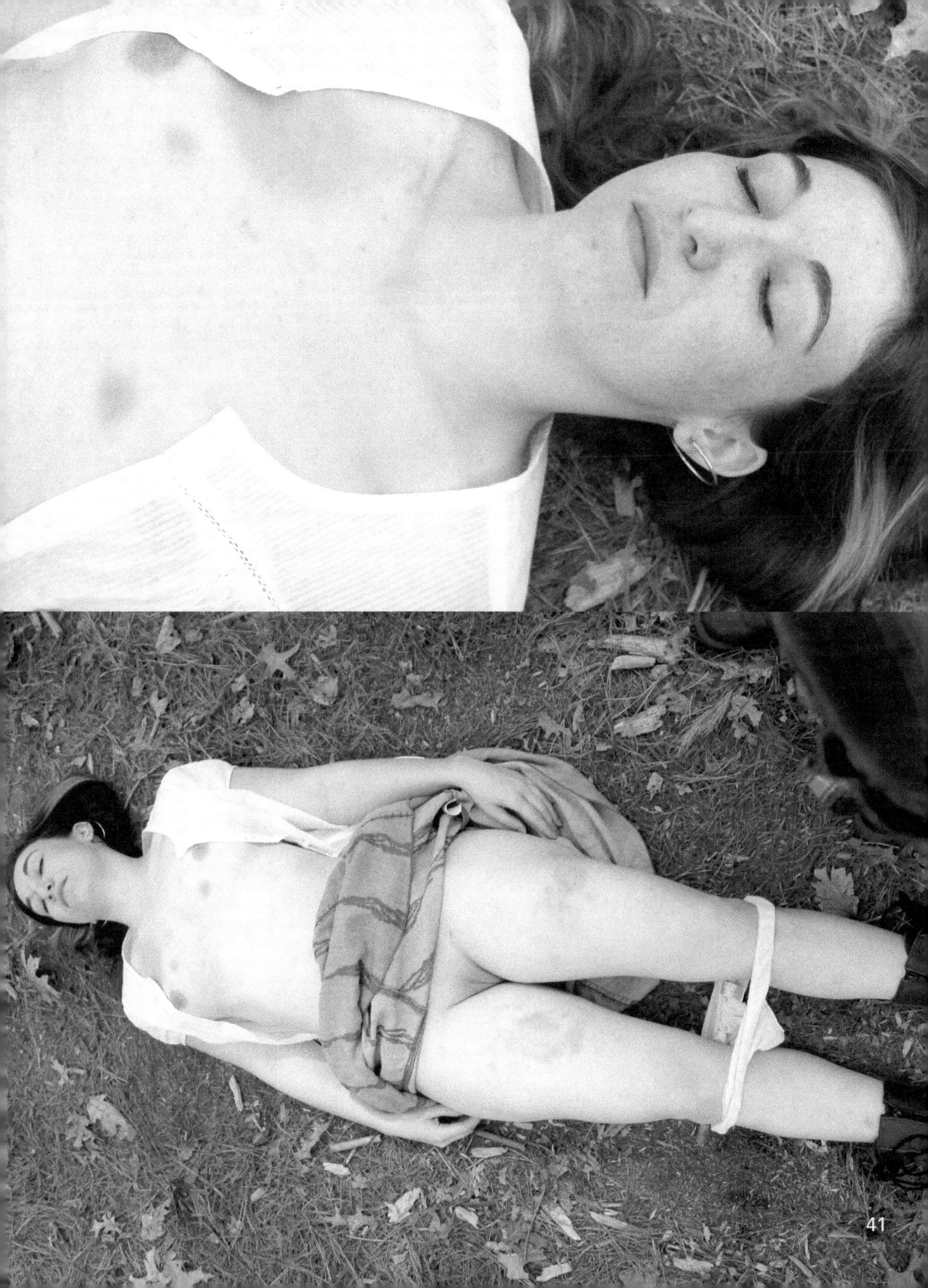

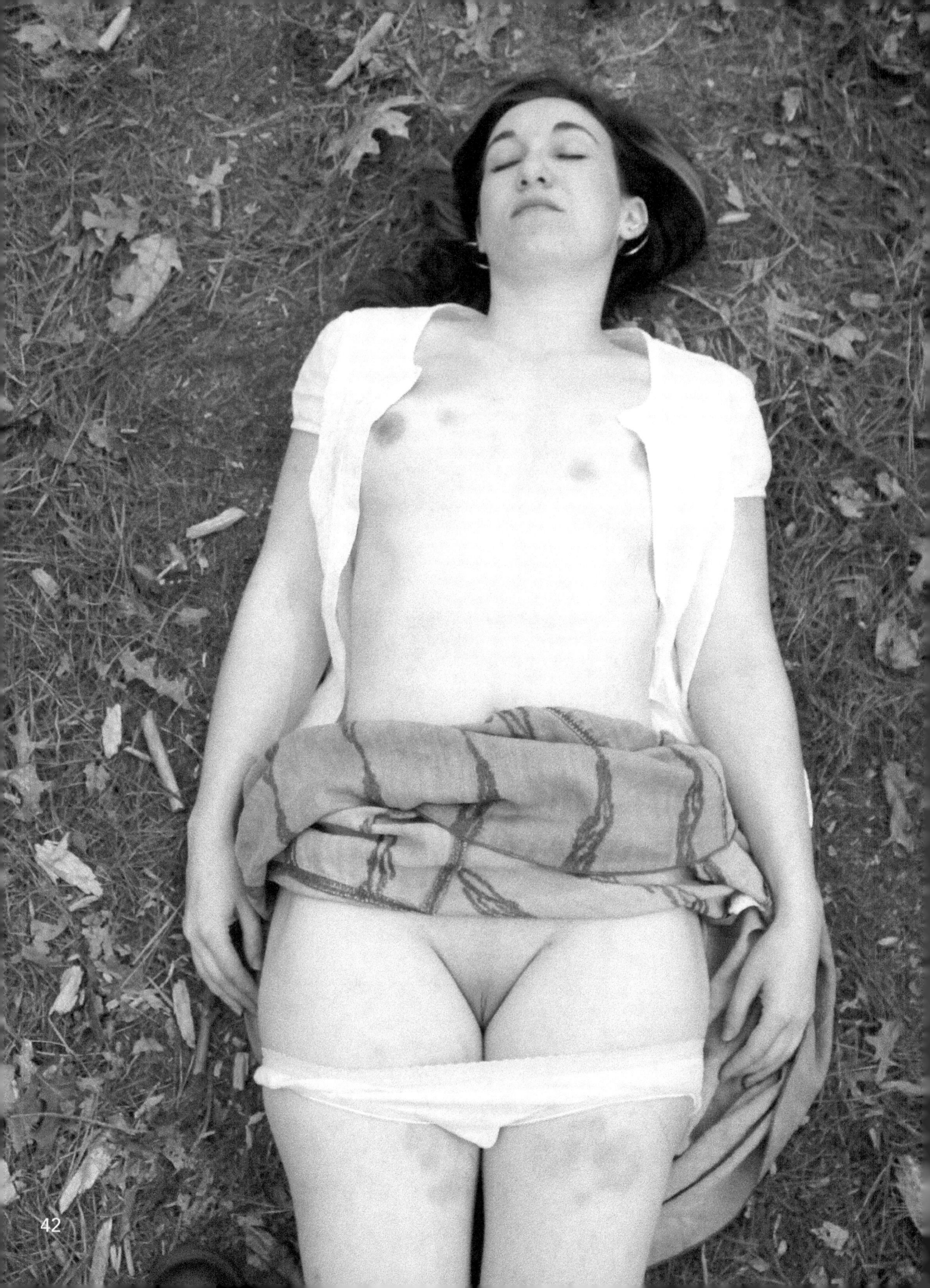

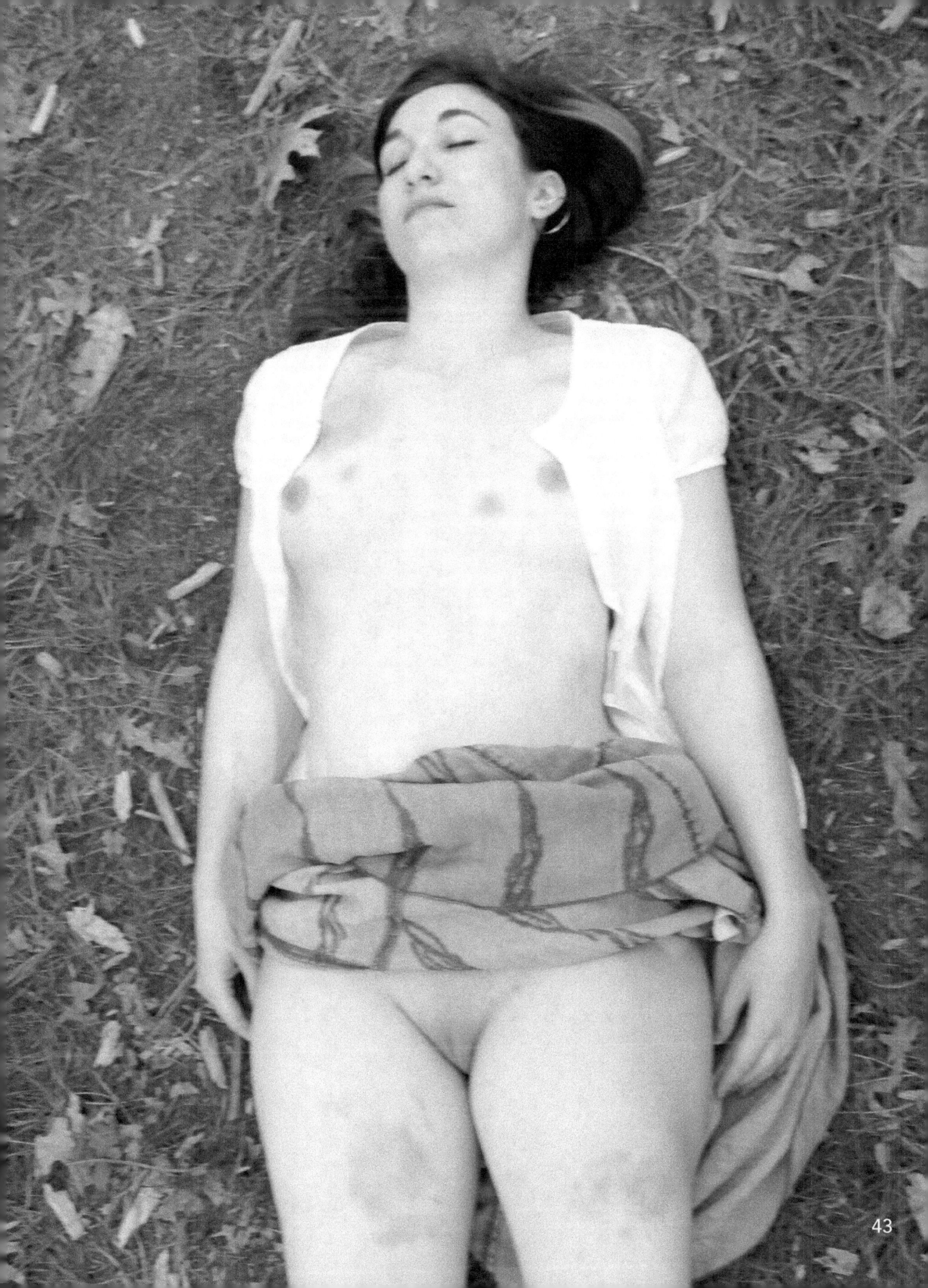

Extras

"Because it's not healthy
to take yourself
too seriously!"

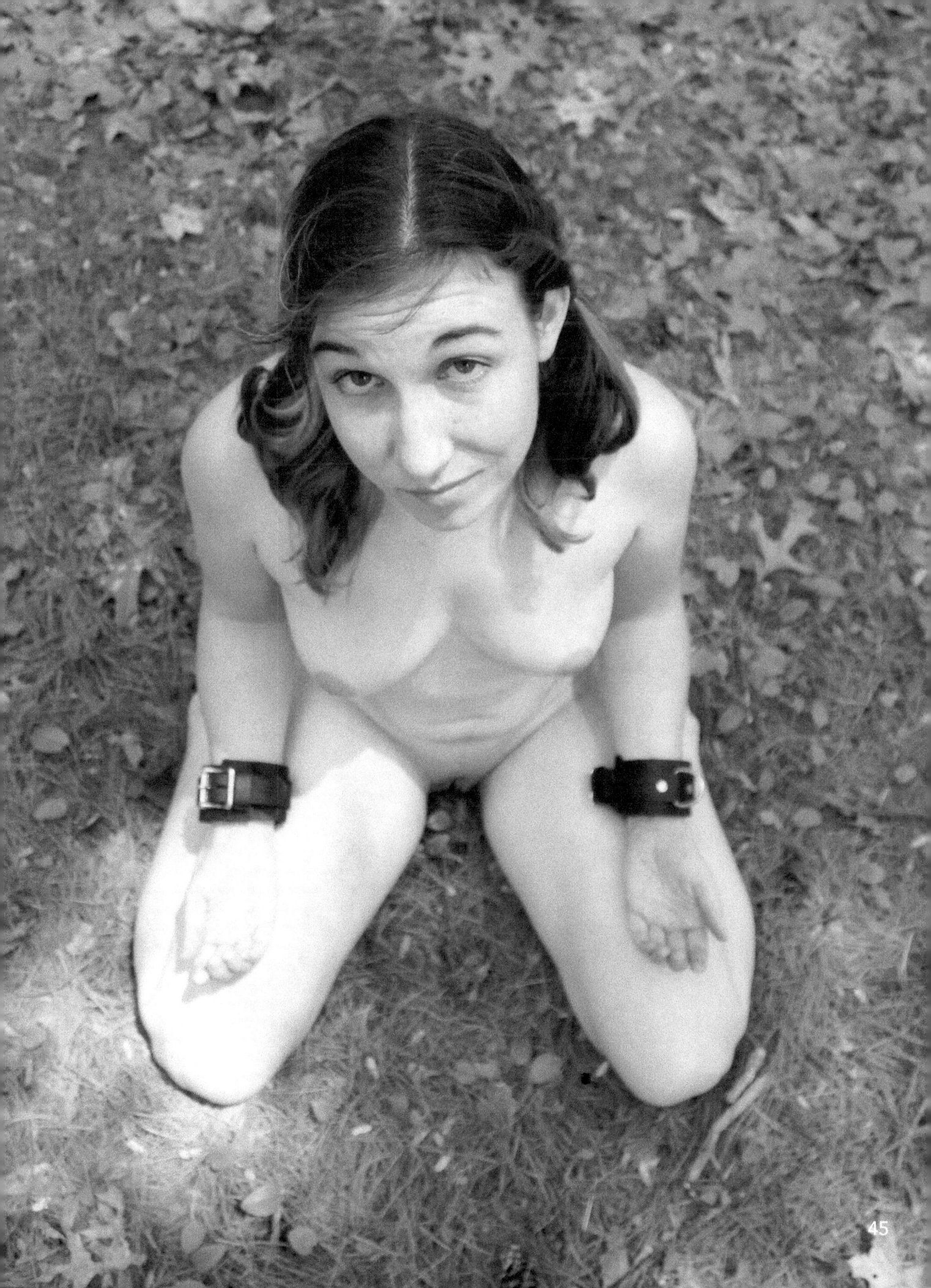

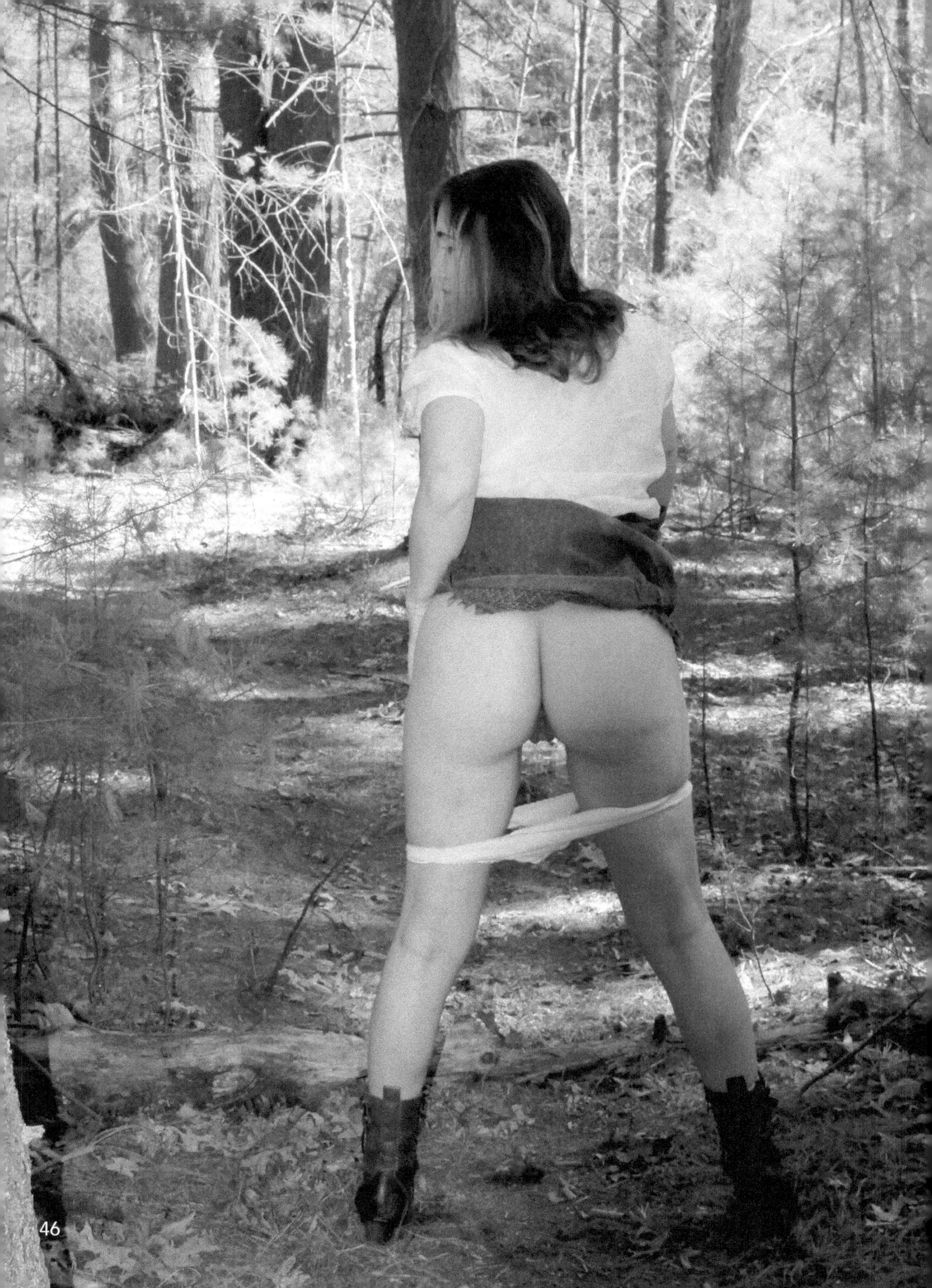

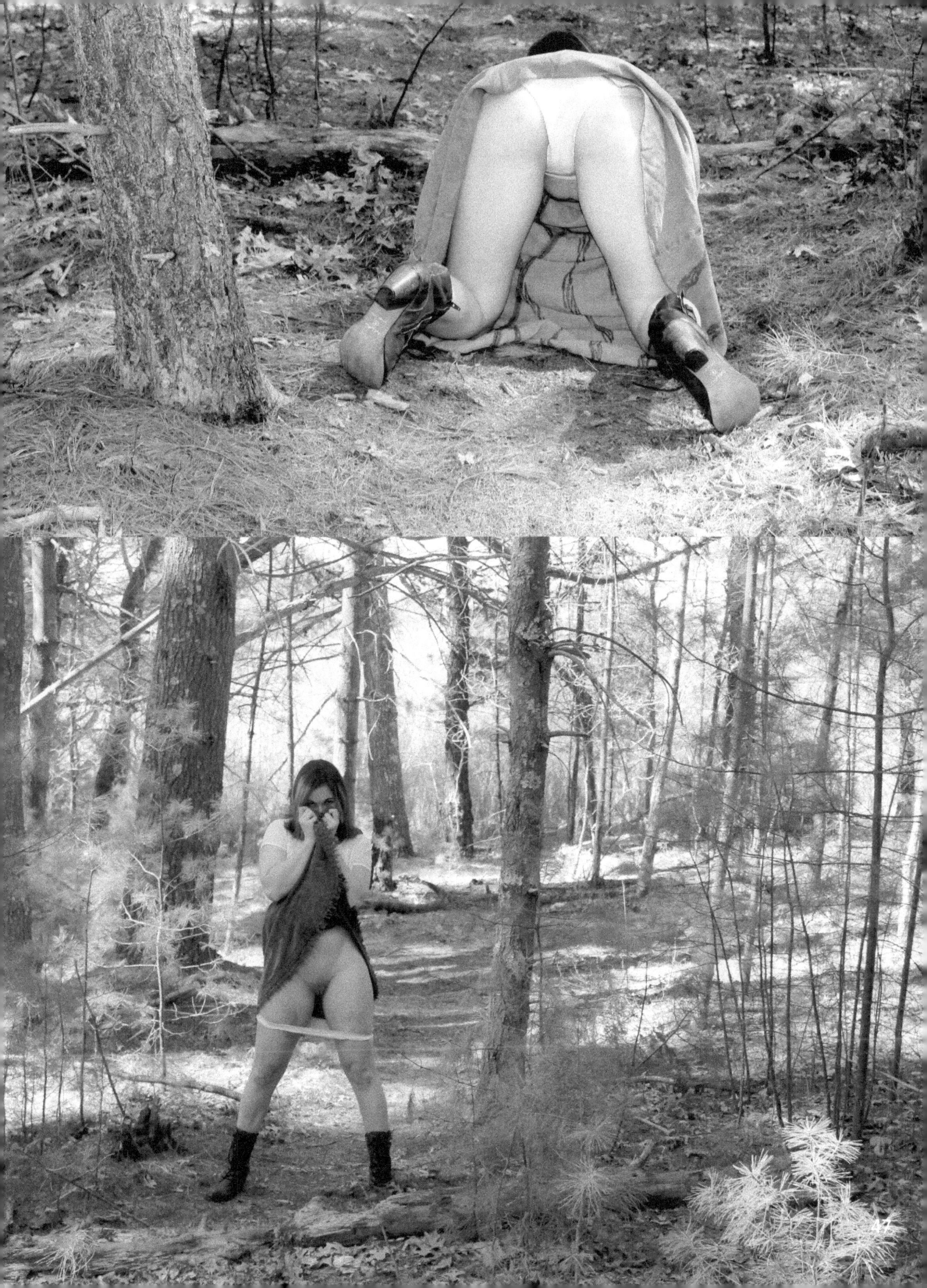

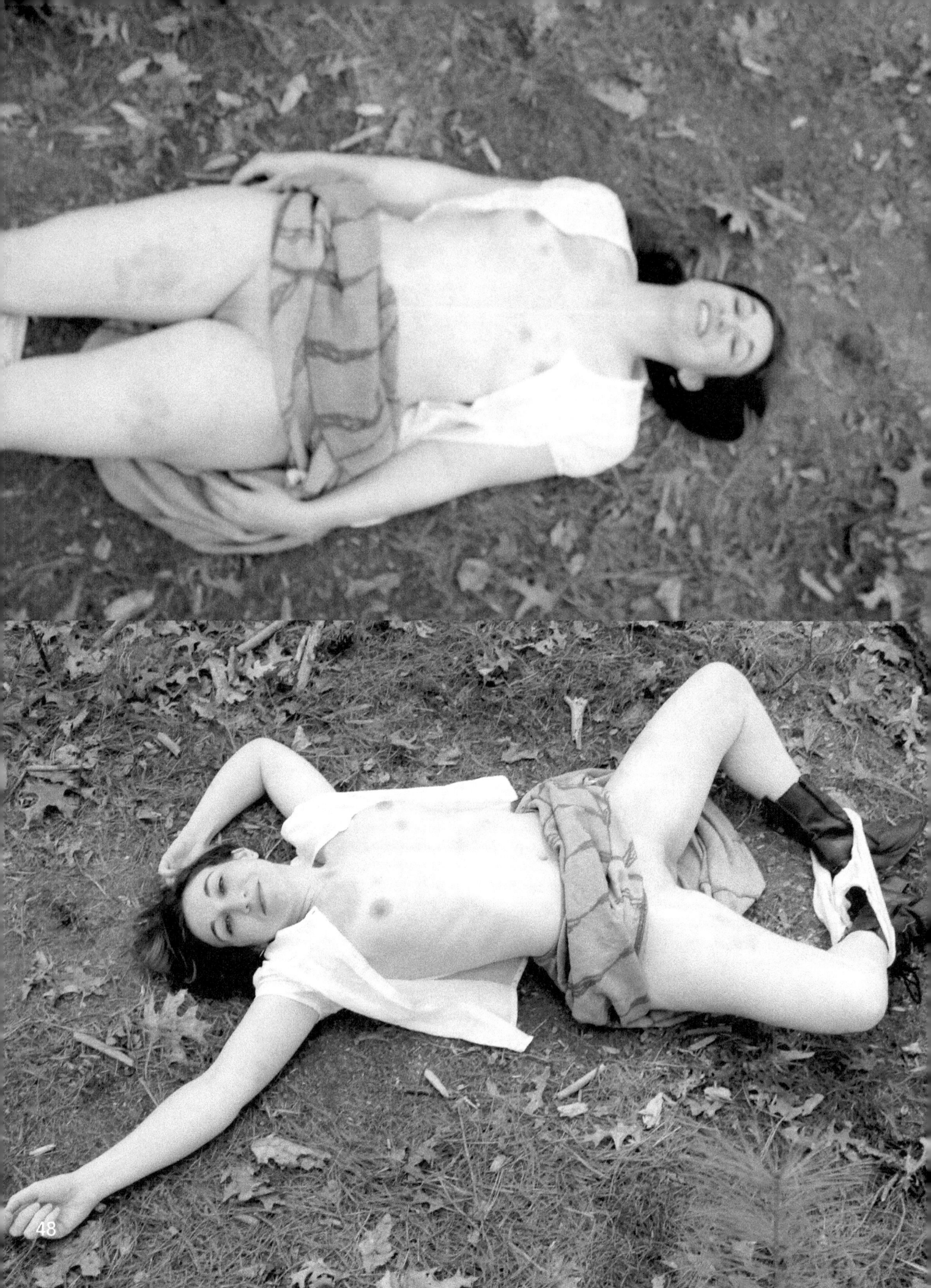

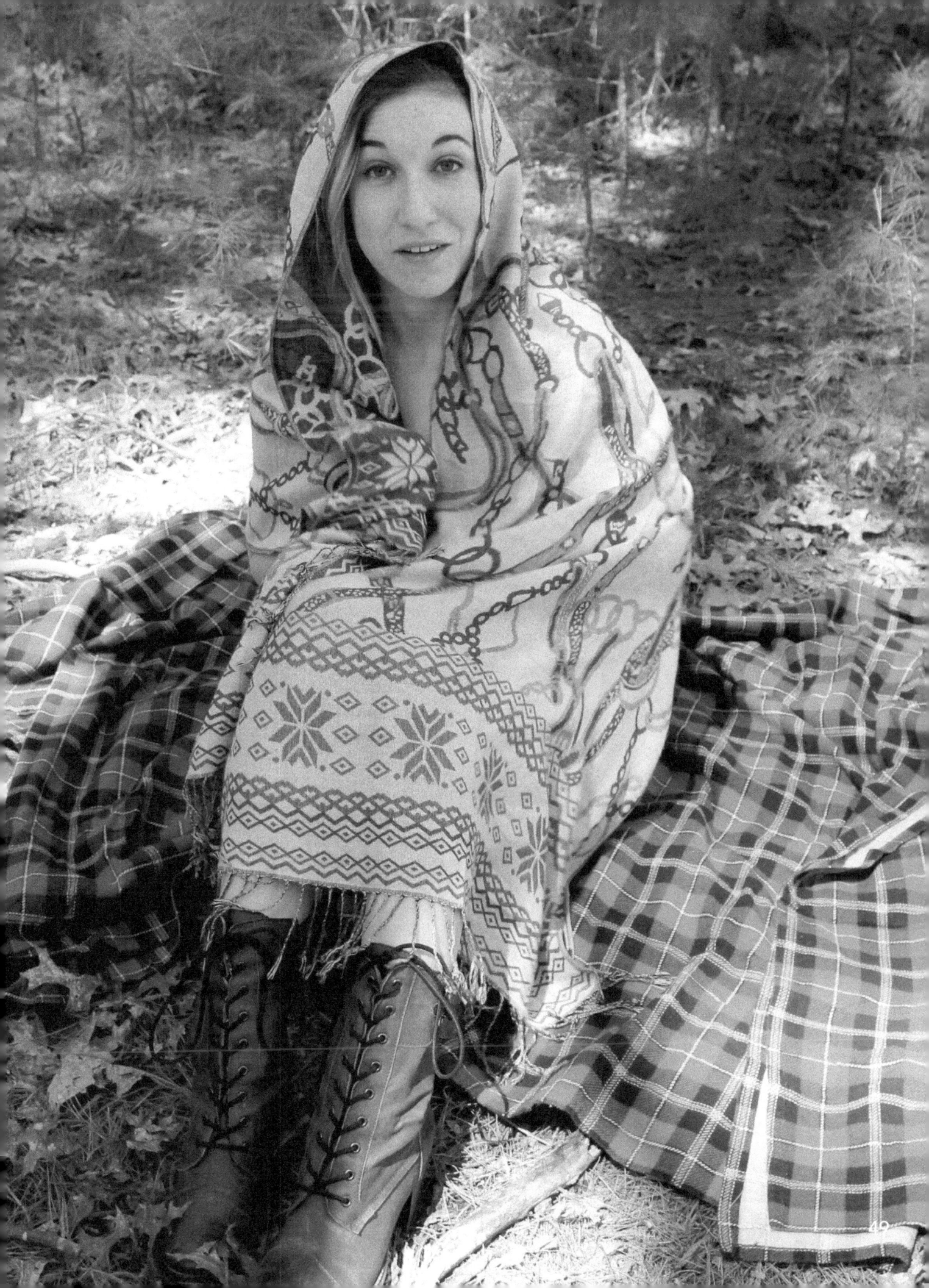

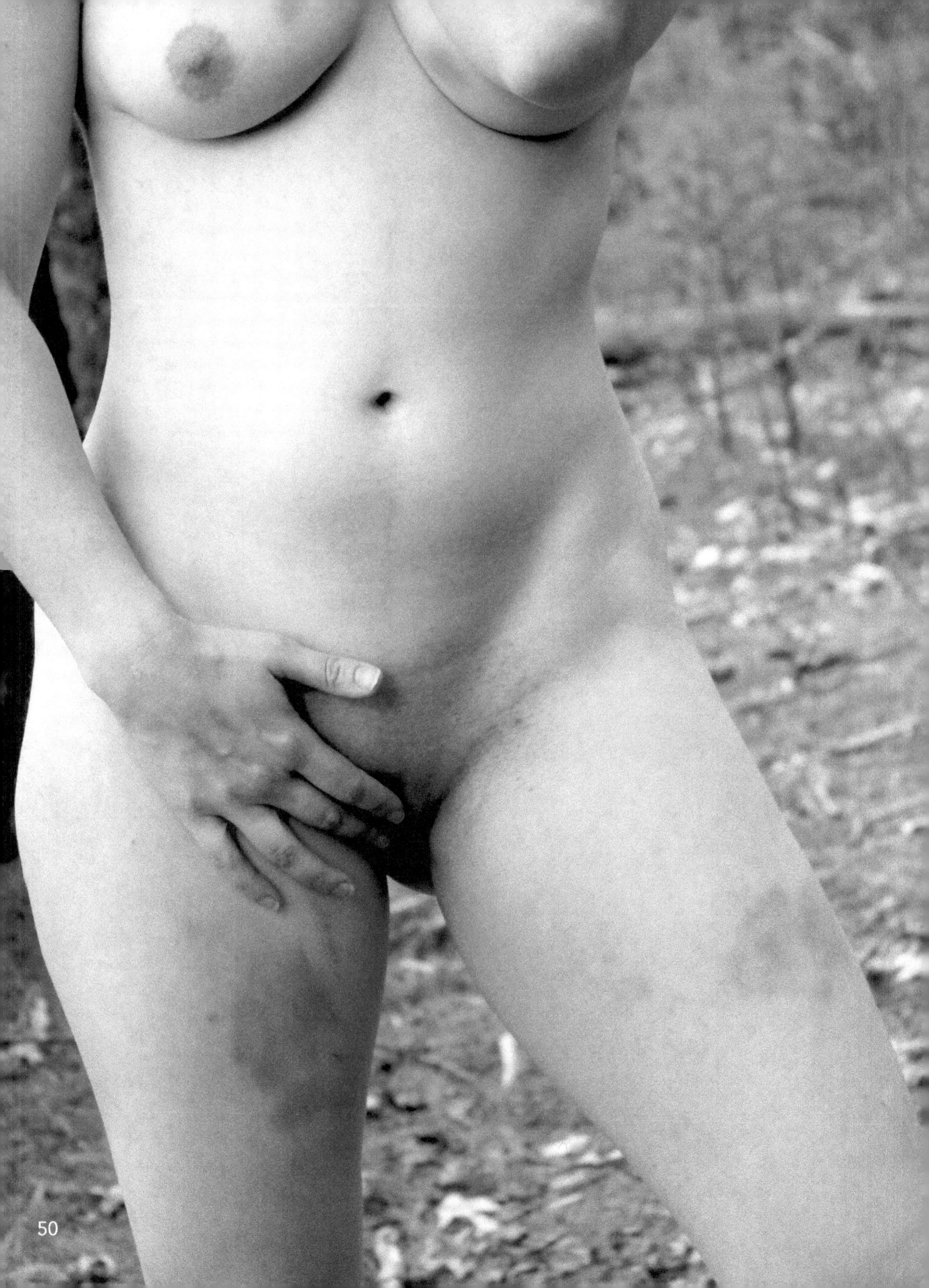

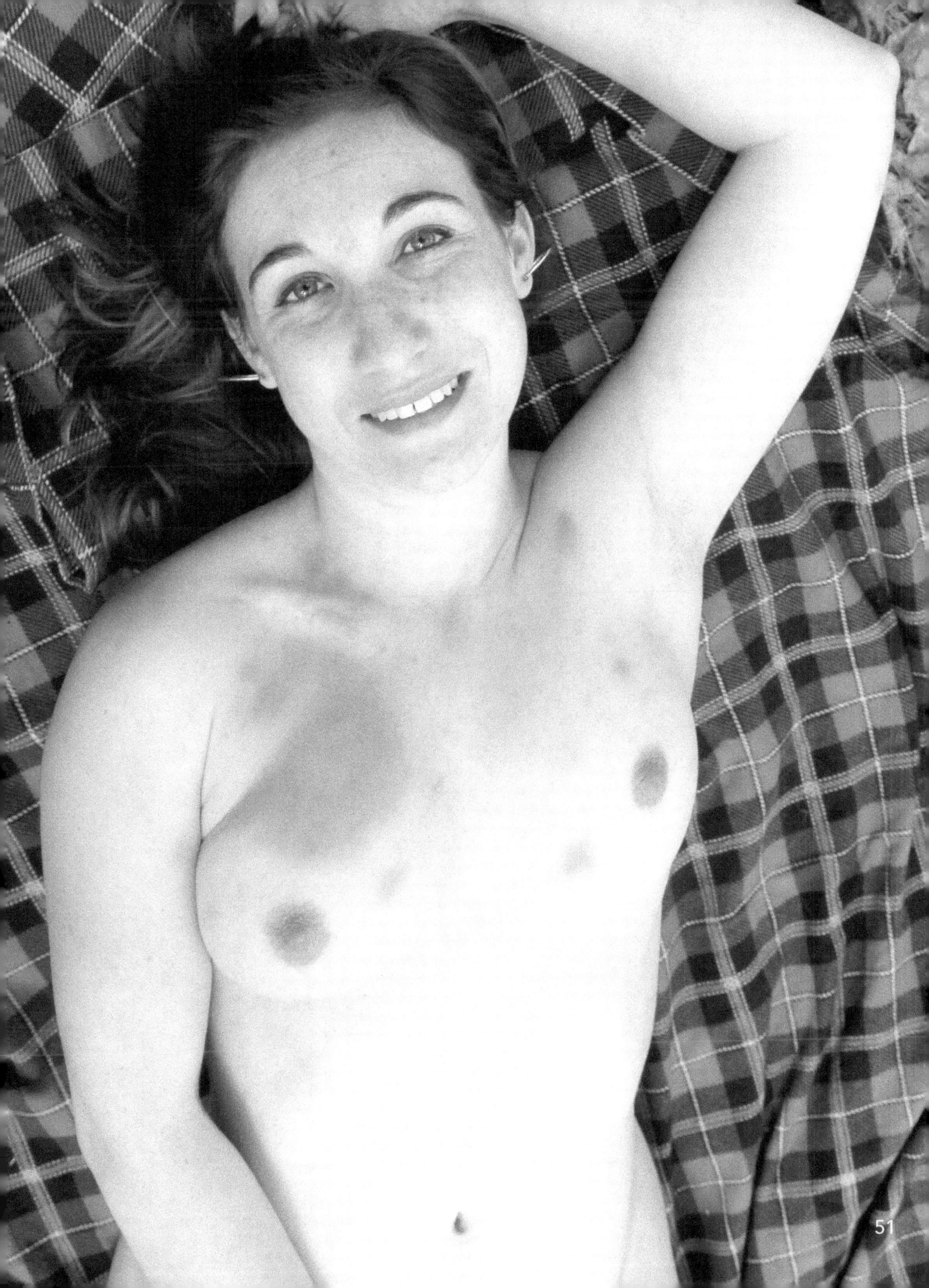

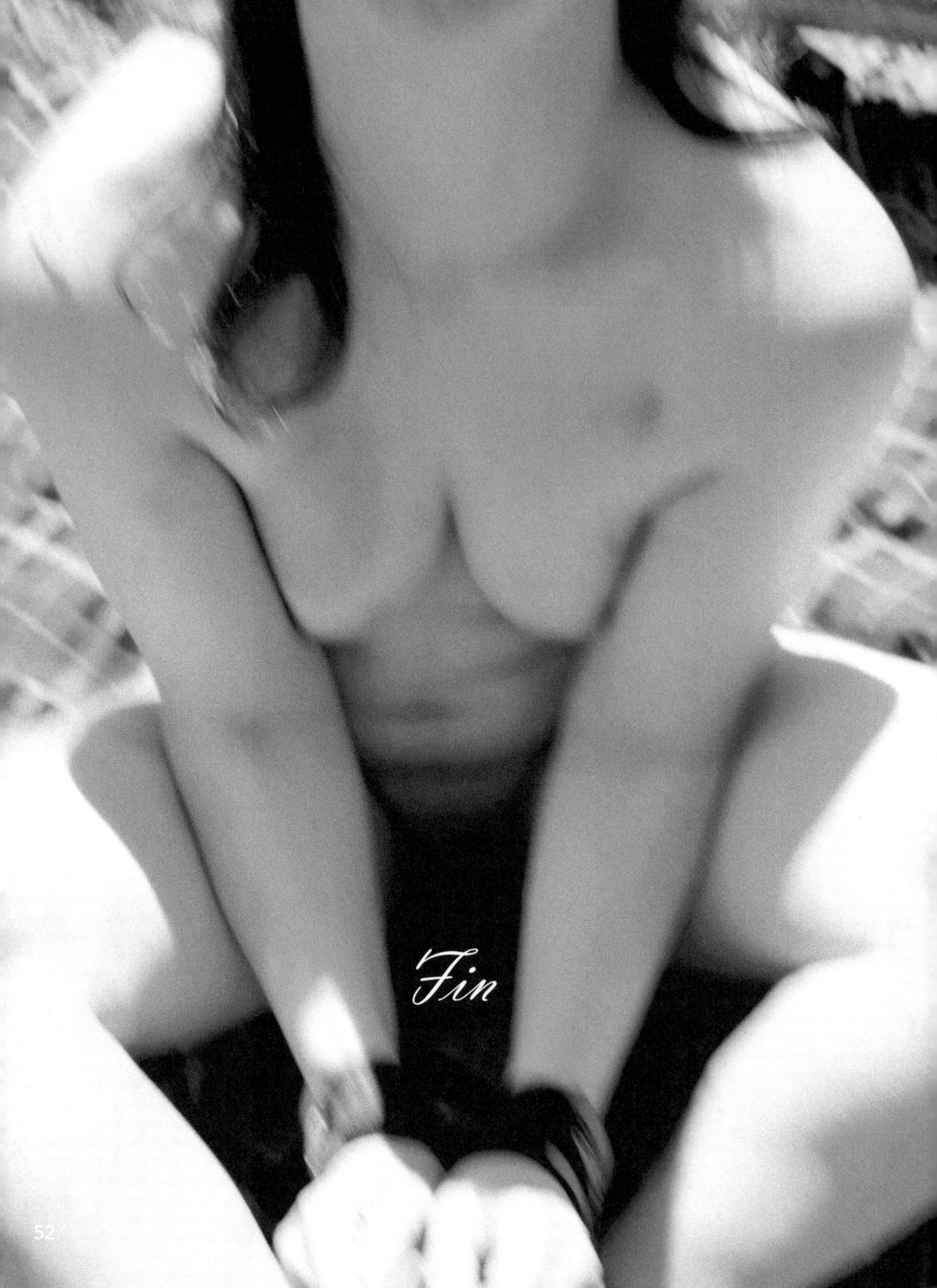

www.ingramcontent.com/pod-product-compliance
Lightning Source LLC
Chambersburg PA
CBHW080608180526
45168CB00007B/2825